D1590777

CONTEMPLATION IN LIBERATION– A METHOD FOR SPIRITUAL EDUCATION IN THE SCHOOLS

CONTEMPLATION IN LIBERATION–
A METHOD FOR SPIRITUAL EDUCATION
IN THE SCHOOLS

Michael Dallaire

Mellen Studies in Education
Volume 56

The Edwin Mellen Press

Library of Congress Cataloging-in-Publication Data

Dallaire, Michael.
   Contemplation in liberation : a method for spiritual education in the schools / Michael Dallaire.
     p. cm. -- (Mellen studies in education ; v. 56)
   Includes bibliographical references and index.
   ISBN 0-7734-7550-8
     1. Education--Aims and objectives. 2. Education--Philosophy. 3. Spiritual life. 4.
Educational sociology. I. Title. II. Series.

LB41 .D215 2001
370.1'14--dc21

                                                    00-064065

> This is volume 56 in the continuing series
> Mellen Studies in Education
> Volume 56 ISBN 0-7734-7550-8
> MSE Series ISBN 0-88946-935-0

A CIP catalog record for this book is available from the British Library.

The Edwin Mellen Press
Box 450
Lewiston, New York
USA 14092-0450

The Edwin Mellen Press
Box 67
Queenston, Ontario
CANADA L0S 1L0

The Edwin Mellen Press, Ltd.
Lampeter, Ceredigion, Wales
UNITED KINGDOM SA48 8LT

Dedicated To

My mother and father
Doreen LeBlond and Maurice Dallaire

and to

Erin Marie Fowler
The one in whom my soul delights.

TABLE OF CONTENTS

PREFACE

The importance of contemplation is beginning to take hold in our consciousness. We often see articles in the media on the value of various forms of meditation and other contemplative practices. As the rush of daily life increases I think the interest in contemplation will continue to rise. The pace of modern life leaves us with few alternatives. We can either let the mad rush take over or we can begin to seek other ways of living. This is the appeal of contemplation in that it provides a sane alternative to the madness of modern life.

Michael Dallaire explores the nature of contemplation in this book within this context. He sees contemplation as a means to living more authentically in the world. Contemplation for Dallaire is not a retreat from the world but an active engagement with the world. Contemplation allows us to live with awareness, sensitivity and compassion.

Dallaire has brought a balanced approach to contemplation that recognizes the importance of both silence and an active, committed life. Dallaire teaches and counsels students in a Catholic secondary school and thus he is one who is in the trenches and is not discussing contemplation from just a theoretical perspective. His working experience helps ground the text and the theory that he articulates.

Although Dallaire works from a Catholic perspective this book should be of value to almost anyone interested in contemplation and spirituality. Dallaire acknowledges the importance of seeing contemplation from a spiritual perspective that is not limited to one particular faith. Again there is balance in the book between his own faith and this broader perspective.

Dallaire's contemplation for liberating praxis is a concept that we very much need in our world. Contemplation has been practiced for centuries in many cultures and traditions and one of the essential goals of contemplation in these various traditions is freedom or liberation. Contemplation can allow us to step back from our social roles and actually experience an awareness that is beyond those roles or an unconditioned self. It is this unconditioned self which is the source of wisdom, love and compassion that we need to cultivate in our schools. I believe the development of contemplation for liberating praxis is much more important than many of the so-called outcomes that Ministries and Departments of Education call for today. If our schools were oriented towards Dallaire's vision rather than just training students to compete in a global economy we would live in a much happier and saner world.

Jack Miller, Ph.D.
The Ontario Institute for Studies in Education
of the University of Toronto

ACKNOWLEDGMENTS

The journey towards completing this book has been a tremendously rewarding experience. It has been a journey that I had to take so as to find my own 'voice' in the midst of the 'melody' being sung today in our world. Although a solitary task, I never felt alone for there were many who supported me along the way. While I cannot mention everyone, there are some who I feel deserve special recognition.

I am grateful for the professors and the students I met at the Ontario Institute for Studies in Education of the University of Toronto. The interest and openness that they showed towards my research topic stimulated and sustained me over the years it took to complete this study. One of the unique characteristics of O.I.S.E. is its interdisciplinary approach and the possibility to meet people with diverse perspectives. This exposure has enriched me immensely.

I am particularly thankful to Professor Clive Beck, for his support throughout this project. His breadths of knowledge and practical wisdom were helpful along the way. He encouraged me to find my own way and gently challenged me at various times. In so doing he guided me through the research process.

A topic such as mine, so closely connected to my personal questions and professional life, is the result of the influence of many people who have contributed to my way of seeing the world. From my mother and father, who raised me within a religious worldview, I learned the importance of caring for self and others and that engagement in both fields of concern is a requirement for authentic personhood. From the Missionary Oblates of Mary Immaculate, with whom I was associated for several years, I first learned about the Ignatian method of contemplation-in-action. From Patricia McCarney and the staff at the Centre for Spiritual Growth in Ottawa

xi

I learned the value of seeing everyday life through contemplative eyes and to appreciate the need for contemplation inside and outside institutional religions. From the people of Foster Farm and Morrison Gardens in Ottawa and the Ottawa West End Community Chaplaincy, who gave me the opportunity to put my dreams into action, I learned many valuable lessons on community and political action. From each of these communities I learned that spirituality can never be private since it always involves community and politics.

For the community of 'kindred spirits' I have met along the way I give thanks. Martin Jeffrey affirmed me as a natural teacher while Dr. Jim Brown reminded me that there are others within the teaching profession who are asking questions like mine. Professors John Van Den Hengel, S.C.J. and Ken Melchin of St. Paul University modeled the best of academic life. Rita Cross, a single mother on social assistance who received the 1986 Ottawa Citizen of the Year award, taught me how to share a cup of tea when times are tough. Fred Magee, O.M.I., a friend and spiritual advisor, supported me when I most needed it and taught me the value of laughter in keeping my spirits up. Andre Guindon, O.M.I., through his life and death witnessed to the importance of the prophetic role for intellectuals within academics. Finally, Susan Evans has been a long time friend and seeker who has shared equally in the contemplative way while engaged in the quest for social justice. For these 'kindred spirits' I give thanks.

Finally, I am thankful to Erin, my lifetime partner, who believed in me and supported me in this journey. Her love has been part of the fertile ground I needed so as to have the strength and courage to accomplish this task. In addition to her patience I valued her insights and critique of my ideas as they emerged and found there way on to the page. While the thoughts and errors in this book are mine, her contribution is easily known. All one has to do is read between the lines.

INTRODUCTION

> To withdraw from the hunt when there is quarry immediately before
> one and postpone the pursuit while giving oneself to the forging of a
> new and vastly superior instrument ... is not the act of a drifter or a
> self-seeker. (Crowe, 1980, p.41)

While I am under no illusions that this book amounts to the creation of a

'vastly superior instrument' I have found the experience of writing this book one of

withdrawing from the hunt. That is, I have pursued this doctoral research on a part-

time basis while working as a chaplain in a Catholic high school in Southeastern

Ontario, Canada. Throughout each course and while researching and writing this

book I have experienced the need to withdraw from my daily work and to reflect

upon my practice always with the view of returning to 'the hunt' with a better view

on how to proceed.

Now, it may be somewhat distasteful to some to use an analogy such as

hunting to refer to education and I would certainly not want to push this analogy too

far. Still, it does point to the realities of: active engagement with students, parents,

and colleagues; the pursuit of knowledge and wisdom; and a depository of skills to

communicate and instruct each of which is part of the overall enterprise of education.

Moreover, to the extent that hunting was absolutely crucial to the survival of the

human species, so too is education absolutely crucial to the survival of our planet

today. The "increasing interdependence of nations and the emergence of so many

problems of global dimension" (King and Schneider, 1991, p.215), require that we

seek to educate with an urgency similar to tribal hunters' need to feed their people.

It is because I see education as having profound personal and social implications that I have valued the opportunity to pursue this level of study. It is also because I see questions pertaining to spirituality as integral to addressing many of the problems facing us in this global age that I have opted to pursue research in the area of education for spirituality.

Personal and Professional Motivations for this Book

There has been a high level of personal motivation behind my research and my writing. Throughout my adult life I have sought to find a balance between my quiet, reflective nature and my active life of pastoral work and teaching. The horizon under which both my reflective and active dimensions have been lived has been the horizon of committed social action on the side of those who are disenfranchised and marginalized within society. I have continually asked how my contemplative nature and my concern for social justice are related as I seek to contribute to a more just society. In a nutshell, on a personal level I have explored an integration of contemplation and action that is socially liberating not only for myself but also for the communities in which I live and work. This book is one expression of this on-going exploration.

Professionally, while I am a certified teacher, I have worked as a chaplain for the last fifteen years in a variety of contexts. My entry into the field of pastoral ministry involved a one year placement as a pastoral associate in a Roman Catholic parish in Labrador, Canada. Very quickly I saw that a parish location was not for me. Consequently, I moved away from the official structure of a church and sought alternative work.

The work that provided the genesis for my topic was the three years during the mid-1980's when I ministered as an ecumenical community chaplain amongst

Ottawa's urban poor. It was then that my questions around the relationship between contemplation and liberating praxis began to be formulated. Indeed, it was only through embracing an approach of being contemplatives in action that a community based chaplaincy program has emerged (Evans and Dallaire, 1989, pp.34-35). What originally was to be a three year pilot project has become a vibrant approach to community chaplaincy that today extends to four public housing projects in Ottawa. Many of the problems addressed and insights discussed here flow from this valuable experience.

The questions I had concerning contemplation and social action continued to surface even when I changed the location for my work and became a Catholic high school chaplain which is what I have been engaged in for over ten years. My first three years in high school chaplaincy were in a poor, rural school in Southern Ontario. The students in that school exhibited a fair degree of sensitivity to the questions of the social implications of one's spirituality. I suspect this was due partly to the students' themselves coming from poorer economic situations. The majority of students, eighty percent, came from farms and villages where, despite the rugged individualism, people were more conscious of their need of others for survival. In that location I gained a heightened appreciation for the importance of community for social action. Indeed, my appreciation of the centrality of community for spirituality, which I had gained while working as an ecumenical chaplain, was confirmed.

For the past eight years I have worked in a suburban, middle class school where I have encountered greater resistance, and often apathy, to the questions of how one's spirituality is related to social justice. Gibson Winter has identified one of the reasons for the inability of suburban communities to respond effectively to the needs of the disadvantaged as being rooted in the fact that people in the suburbs tend to seek community among people of similar economic status. Winter, writing about urban churches, argues that when the gravitation towards homogeneous communities based on economic status is coupled with privatized religion what results is a situation in which suburban churches seem incapable of responding to social justice concerns (Winter, 1961, pp.135-155). I see the effects of these two factors, economic homogeneity and privatism, in my school whenever I seek to connect the concerns of spiritual life with political and social justice concerns. My immersion in a suburban context has caused me to reflect deeper on some of the philosophical and cultural problems associated with trying to educate for a spirituality that includes social and political action. Many of my reflections are expressed throughout this book which is an attempt to propose a method for a politically responsive spirituality that is life-giving for both individuals and communities.

Locating Myself Within Education

It is important that I locate myself within my social context. First, I am a white, educated male who is in the middle of my life. Despite the privilege of being white and male the concerns for gender and marginalization are woven into my topic. Second, while I identify myself first and foremost as a Canadian, my familial roots are Irish peasantry and French Canadian working class. These familial roots help explain my sensitivity to the impact of social and economic life on people, which is an important element of my topic. Third, I am a middle class professional, one generation removed from the laboring class on my father's side and several generations removed from the immigrant farmers on my mother's side. This has given me a deep appreciation of the need for justice in economics and in the ecology. Fourth, my religious background is Roman Catholic. This religious bias will be evident throughout my book for although I seek to propose a method for spiritual education that is interreligious as well as available to non-religious persons, I admit that I am indebted to the contemplative-in-action method that comes out of the Roman Catholic tradition. Moreover, I identify my Catholic background as the source of the organicism that permeates my book as I seek to provide a method for spiritual education that is holistic.

While I am working as a high school chaplain with an academic background in history, philosophy, and theology, I have deliberately chosen to write a philosophy of education work rather than a theological work for several reasons. First, I am presently working in a school. If I am to speak intelligently about spirituality it is imperative that I know the 'language' of educators and the concerns of people who are involved in schooling. Therefore, while this book proposes a method for spiritual education that can be used beyond formal education systems, it is necessary that my proposal hold currency for educators within schools today. I believe that approaching the topic of spirituality through the door of philosophy of education will give my method a degree of credibility within educational circles.

Second, I see schools as locations for exploring the larger questions that are being played out in our culture. In this sense, the school in which I presently work functions as a window to Western culture. Thus, the philosophical and spiritual questions that are operative in our culture today are present within schools simply because schools function within society. As such, I believe that I can come at the larger cultural questions through an exploration of philosophy of education. Indeed, attending to the social, cultural, and political concerns of our time is integral to my entire topic.

Third, although I serve in a high school as a chaplain, I see myself first and foremost as an educator. While I am not a classroom teacher, I am intimately involved in the life of the school through my daily interactions with students, teachers, administrators, and parents. This interaction has required an acute sensitivity to the concerns of professional educators and students. It has also required that I be fairly cognizant of the changes within schools that are taking place and to be able to discuss the philosophical concerns underlying these changes.

Finally, I see education as much more than formal schooling although the years of primary and secondary education are crucial. Education is a life-long process beginning before kindergarten and lasting long after formal schooling. This work seeks to provide a method of education for spiritual formation that can be followed throughout one's entire life. As such, the method I propose here can be useful within schools but is also a method that can be followed throughout life and in a variety of locations.

Choosing the Focus of Spirituality and Education

Catholic education has traditionally stood upon a triad structure of home, school, and parish (Pead, 1992, p.9), and much of the Catholic reflection on education presumes this triad. However, this triad relationship has deteriorated to such an extent and for a variety of reasons that it now only functions as an organizational framework for a minority of those who are engaged in Catholic education. Moreover, while Catholic education may offer a worldview that challenges the surrounding culture (Leddy, 1991, pp.19-33), it is my observation that this worldview speaks to only a minority today. My concern as a chaplain has not been to deliberate over the future of Catholic education in Ontario as Mulligan as done in his work on Catholic education (Mulligan, 1999). While this is a pressing need I have opted to focus on my primary concern, which has been to encourage others to grow in their spiritual life. As a result, my questions have not been questions concerning religious education and the need to master content, rituals, morals, and doctrines, which are the concerns of religious educators. My focus has been on spirituality and how I can best educate for a healthy and comprehensive spiritual life. Hence, while there are overlaps between religion and spirituality I have chosen to focus specifically on education for spirituality.

The need to provide an education for spirituality is an emerging field of study within education. Certainly, religious educators such as Thomas Groome, Sofia Cavalletti, Thomas Del Prete, and Maria Harris have sought to provide pedagogies for spiritual education. Recently, however, there are a growing number of non-religious educators who have been arguing that we need to educate for the spiritual dimension of life. Clive Beck, James Moffett, Nel Noddings, and Parker Palmer represent educators outside the explicitly religious realm who argue for spiritual education and seek to integrate spirituality within educational practice. Moreover, substantial work has occurred in the areas of meditation and contemplation within education, which is a major part of my book. Jack Miller, Susan Drake, and Margret Buchmann have argued for an approach to spiritual education that fosters the inner life of a person through meditation, visualization, and contemplation. Finally, the question of spirituality has become so important that it has become a bit of an administrative 'hot potato'. In a recent issue of "Educational Leadership" (Dec. 1998), twelve articles dealt explicitly with the question of the need to include education for spirituality within public schools. Although this journal is written from the context of the United States, Canadians are not immune to the issue. Indeed, Lois Sweet in her recent book *God in the Classroom* (1997), has outlined both the historical and contemporary debate around religion in Canadian schools. While Sweet does not deal directly with questions concerning spirituality, as distinct from religion, I suspect that the complexity of the controversy of teaching for spirituality within Canadian schools would be comparable to the one she describes about teaching religion. Furthermore, my suspicion is that this discourse regarding education and spirituality, which is emerging in Canada, can be found in other parts of the world where the questions of education, morals, religion, and spirituality are being pursued.

So, there is a growing body of research and discourse on the question of education for spirituality within schools today. Much of this has been commendable. However, there are two weaknesses that I have noticed. First, educational thinkers who have written from a secular or non-religious stance have not been able to tap into the well of experience in educating for a spiritual life that formal religions could provide. My book, in its attempts to reconstruct the traditional method of contemplation-in-action seeks to avoid this oversight. Secondly, most educators for spirituality, whether religious or non-religious, tend not to make a strong connection between spirituality and action for social change. At best, social and political implications of spirituality are secondary to their methods. My book seeks to overcome this deficiency and to bring the concerns of social and political action directly into the discussion on spirituality. In fact, I see social and political action as a necessary constitutive component of spirituality if it is to be credible in our world today.

A Question of Method

My concern is not so much with the attributes or qualities to be associated with a spiritual person although these are important. Rather, I am more concerned with articulating a life-affirming, holistic, and socially responsive method for spiritual education for our times. As such, I propose a method for education in spirituality that makes explicit the connection between contemplation and actions for liberation. Religions have traditionally taught that contemplation and action function best in an interdependent and balanced fashion. While this method may be correct, it needs to be reconstituted for the challenges of our time. The challenges, which will be discussed, require that we widen our understanding of contemplation and of action. The core question that forms the backdrop for my reflections throughout this work is, "how can we best educate for contemplation and liberating praxis within North America today?". That is, can contemplation and action be intelligently pursued in our culture and if so, how?

My method moves beyond the theocentric and anthropocentric focuses of traditional religious approaches to spirituality. I do not discount these loci but find that we need to broaden our understanding of spirituality so as to include the insights of secular humanists, feminists, ecologist, and holistic educators. The reason I seek to include these insights is that I think that some of the finest insights for educating for a spiritual life come from individuals who would not call themselves religious, from feminists who reject patriarchal religion, from ecologists who sound the alarm concerning the growing global environmental crisis, and from holistic educators who are proposing inclusive pedagogies. These insights are necessary correctives to the traditional approaches to spiritual life as centered on a transcendent, male God who rules the universe.

I value the place of action not as a secondary by-product of personal piety but as a constitutive element of a truly holistic spirituality. I presume that the social structures in which we live and how we engage with these structures are integral to spirituality. Hence, a person who is committed to liberating actions or social transformation ought to feel that their engagement is a full partner in their spiritual life. Likewise, the reflective, contemplative dimension of life needs to be brought fully into our social and political engagement. In this work I have sought to articulate a method that promotes a holistic dialectic between the contemplative dimension and the active dimension of liberating praxis. I believe that such a method can have currency for educators today both in and outside formal educational systems.

Research Methodology

My research method is quite traditional in that I discuss the current theoretical discourse on my topic. Hence, I appeal to primary sources and to key thinkers. However, I do not stay within only one field of discourse but rather weave together several fields. I appeal to the contributions from educational theory, religious education, critical pedagogy, liberation theology, philosophy, and traditional spiritual education. While I seek to write from a North American perspective I do at times borrow from the insights that have arisen from European and Latin American locations.

Moreover, since my hope is that my book can be useful to both religious and non-religious educators, I judge the ideas of thinkers based on their merit and contribution to understanding questions of spiritual life as lived within North America today. This requires that I focus on the essential problems and foundational issues concerning education for spirituality. What results is a method for spiritual education that has some plausibility for North American educators seeking to promote a spirituality that is socially responsible.

This book was originally written as a dissertation in the philosophy of education and as a result it is mainly theoretical. However, I use my pastoral experience as a chaplain, my present location of a high school, and my personal concern for social justice and spirituality as the basis to judge the theoretical content explored. Consequently, I continually keep my eye on how the theory impacts upon praxis and vice versa. Moreover, this concern for the practical issues of education receives considerable attention in the final chapter.

Structure

There are five chapters to this book. The first chapter forms the foundation for the entire method. In it I situate my proposal for a reconstruction of the traditional method of contemplation-in-action within the larger context of postmodernism and the main contemporary challenges to traditional spirituality. I also explore the philosophical impediments within education today that undermine education for spirituality despite the growing call for such an education. Having done this I introduce contemplation-in-action as a credible method for spiritual education but one that needs to be broadened so as to be truly life-affirming and socially responsive.

The second chapter is devoted to exploring the contemplative dimension of human life. This exploration involves a look at mysticism and contemplation as traditionally understood. I then articulate how contemplation understood as 'wonderstruck beholding' is an innately human spirituality and hence available to all regardless of one's religious affiliation or lack thereof. How contemplation is related to holistic education and to the active life is also discussed.

The third chapter is given over to a discussion of the active dimension of social and political action. I address the questions of justice and the need for an appropriate cosmology from which to pursue justice. In light of this liberating praxis is presented as a constitutive component of spirituality and as a necessary requirement for a holistic approach to life.

The fourth chapter is crucial for my proposed method for in it I explain how the two dimensions of life, contemplation and liberating praxis, function together to create a healthy holism. I argue that we need to move beyond the polarization of these two dimensions to an appreciation of the dialectic between the two. This dialectic provides a healthy and holistic approach to living.

In the final chapter I turn towards the practical issues that need to be considered in using my proposed method. I outline strategies for facilitating contemplation and liberating praxis, which are best pursued within community. I discuss the relationship between teachers and students and how both can become contemplatives-in-liberating praxis. Finally, I discuss the possibilities and challenges within various locations for using this method of spiritual education.

Conclusion

Permit me to return to the analogy of the hunt for a moment to help situate this work. While on a hunt there are times when one needs to set up camp and build a fire to cook food and to keep warm. When building a fire, one first gathers wood. Often, one has to search in the woods and the fields to find pieces of wood. Writing this book has been like gathering pieces of wood for the fire. I have looked for ideas that have stood the test of time, for as it is that dry, hard wood makes the best fire, so it is that ideas that have been tested and proven worthy are best included into a study such as this. But, just as smaller pieces of softwood are required to serve as kindling to get a fire going, so it is that newer ideas can spark new life into old ideas. Hence, I have sought to include the new with the old so as to enkindle new life into an old method. My book, then, seeks to propose a method for spiritual education that is responsive to the personal and social concerns of our time. Education is a worthy undertaking and, like hunting was to our ancestors, a necessary work for the survival of our world. This work is offered as one method for spiritual education today. Perhaps it will provide some heat and some energy to sustain educators intend upon educating for a spiritual life in a complex and ever-changing world.

✳

CHAPTER ONE
CONTEMPLATION-IN-LIBERATING PRAXIS IN THE CONTEXT OF CONTEMPORARY SPIRITUALITY AND EDUCATION

> In fact, we 'think' with the debris and the offspring resulting from the wreckage of these systems and perhaps–of the dreams which these systems brought to language.
>
> (Ricoeur, 1975, p.132)

Educators are practical philosophers in that they engage in their practice of teaching based on some philosophy or composite of philosophies. Very often the philosophical ideas that shape their practice have been borrowed from thinkers both old and new. Rarely does a teacher espouse a philosophy that is entirely new or unique. Hence, regardless of whether one is a generalist or a specialist there is a set of philosophical ideas that undergirds one's teaching. This philosophical undergirding applies especially to the area of spirituality, which is the concern of this book, for we understand and express our spiritual lives with the philosophical tools that are available to us.

There are two main concerns that are interwoven throughout this chapter: i) to outline the philosophical landscape in which today's teachers in North America are practicing and, ii) to discuss the area of education for spirituality. Both concerns will be discussed with the view of introducing the traditional Ignatian method of contemplation-in-action as a credible model for spiritual education if it is reframed in light of our contemporary world. This chapter, then, forms the foundation of my

13

theory, which is that contemplation-in-liberating praxis is a valuable method for education in the spiritual life today.

This chapter is divided into four sections. In the first section I provide an overview of postmodernism which is impacting upon North American culture in many ways. I then discuss some of the contemporary North American challenges to traditional spirituality. These include secular humanism, feminism, ecologism, and holism. The third section involves a discussion of education and spirituality. Hence, I discuss the need for spiritual education, outline some obstacles to educating for spirituality, offer my definition of spirituality, and handle the problem of unity and pluralism as it pertains to spirituality. In the final section I put forth my proposal that contemplation-in-liberating praxis is a credible method for spiritual education today.

The Landscape of Postmodernism

William Johnston argues that scholasticism, which formed the philosophical basis for Catholic theology and much of Western culture, no longer holds a monopoly on the explanation of our world (Johnston, 1987, pp.34-35). Indeed, while there remain remnants of this Euro-centric and medieval philosophy within our culture, the reality is "the era of Scholasticism has ended" (Johnston, 1987, p.34), and we are in a new time in which the philosophical landscape has changed dramatically. Today, North American culture is undergoing a profound shift from modernism to postmodernism. Such a shift deserves attention not only because of its importance for understanding contemporary life but also because of the impact which these changes have upon education.

Many authors (Griffin, 1988a, p. x; McKay, 1994, p.32; McGowan, 1991, pp.1-5) describe postmodernism as a general philosophical orientation that has emerged in reaction to the limits of modernity. Modernity, which developed since the Enlightenment, was founded on the root metaphor of the machine. That is, the "Galilean-Cartesian-Baconian-Newtonian science" canon championed the view of mechanization (Griffin, 1988a, pp. x-xi). Within modernity secularism sought to replace religion as the foundation of society (Griffin, 1988a, p. xiii). Moreover, in the modern world the focus was on the autonomous individual, the domination of nature, progress, determinism, relativism, centralization, bureaucracy, differentiation, liberal capitalism, and materialism. With respect to religion, God was best kept out of this world, especially out of the public political realm, and masculine spirituality and patriarchy were to be considered normative. Indeed, the modern world was hostile towards religious traditions and sympathetic towards technology as the modern secular religion (Holland, 1988, pp.42-46). In modernity, society was supposed to move away from supernaturalism and dualism to atheism and materialism (Griffin, 1988b, pp.3-8). Modern consciousness promoted fragmentation and competition, freedom from nature and religion, rationalism, professionalism, and technology. A final and perhaps the most distinguishing feature of modern Western culture was the championing of the autonomous individual (Taylor, 1991, pp.2-4). In light of the medieval worldview which upheld authoritarianism and communalism in both the church and the state, modernity's deliberate move away from control, absolutism, and suppression towards autonomy is quite understandable. In many ways it is commendable for as Taylor has argued, "modern freedom was won by our breaking loose from older moral horizons" (Taylor, 1991, p.3).

Griffin has argued that postmodernism is a diffused movement which seeks to go beyond the limits of modernity (Griffin, 1988a, p. x). While the term 'postmodernism' itself is complex, contentious, and open to various interpretations there are some general characteristics that postmodernists share. Some of these characteristics are so easily recognizable in Western culture today that one could argue that postmodernity rather than modernity is the tenor of our times.

Authors reflecting upon postmodernism agree that one of its main characteristics is anti-foundationalism (McGowan, 1991, p.192; Beck, 1994, pp.4-5, 1995, p.130; White, 1991, pp.115-117; Johnson, 1995, p.79). That is, it is held that there are no universally normative foundations to society. This anti-foundationalism is found in those postmodernist philosophers, in particular Lyotard, who distrust the claim of meta-narratives to be universal (McGowan, 1991, pp.25-28). This distrust of meta-narratives pertains not only to cultural myths and stories but also to philosophies that absolutize or schematize the human condition into neat packages.

Pluralism, diversity, and innovation are common features of postmodernism (Beck, 1995, pp.127-130; McGowan, 1991, pp.59-61). These are in keeping with postmodernism's reaction against modernity's tendency towards universal principles that suppress plurality and heterogeneity in favor of unity and homogeneity (White, 1991, p.117). The desire behind the pursuit of pluralism, diversity, and innovation can be located in the modern reaction to totalitarian systems both secular and religious (Griffin, 1988a, p. x). As a consequence, postmodernism stresses race, gender, and ethnic background as constitutive components to individual and collective 'voices' that are required within a new pluralism (McKay, 1994, p.34).

The concept of incommensurability is another feature of postmodernism. Incommensurability results from the condition of an individual's being so embedded in his/her particular culture, context, or bias (White, 1991, p.118; McGowan, 1991, p.40), that true and authentic dialogue between individuals from different cultures, contexts, and biases is extremely difficult if not impossible. Differences that are sourced in race, gender, and ethnicity account for the difficulties in communication and for the misunderstandings operative in our world. Incommensurability supports pluralism. When operative in conjunction with today's trend away from bureaucracy and hierarchy and toward commitment to decentralized democracies lived out in local situations (Holland, 1988, p.59), incommensurability adds to the pluralism that marks our times.

Postmodernism is usually anti-authoritarian. Such anti-authoritarianism is rooted in a comprehensive understanding of the individual. Rather than the modern Western vision of the autonomous individual who stands alone, postmodernism posits the individual whose identity is related to the community in which the self is found. Most postmodernists reject the idea of a universal, unchanging, unified self in favor of a self that is culturally and communally constituted (Beck, 1995, pp.130-131). The self continually evolves due to intersubjectivity and culture and this creative self contributes to cultural pluralism and to diversity.

McKay has argued that postmodernism arose in reaction to the failure of modernity to deliver on its agenda of justice, freedom, and equality (McKay, 1994, p.32). Thus, rather than reified principles justice needs to be reformulated in a more pluralistic fashion and rooted in the concrete lives of individuals and communities. Hence, universal declarations of human rights and freedoms, which are the legacy of the modern project, will fail to achieve real justice until they are concretized in actual lived situations. Such concretization cannot come about through principles articulated from distanced political bodies. The concretization of the values of justice, freedom, and equality must be achieved through individuals working and living within communities committed to these values (White, 1991, pp.116-118). As a result it is solidarity which postmodernists appeal to as essential for the promotion of justice, freedom, and equality.

Anti-foundationalism, pluralism, diversity, incommensurability, anti-authoritarianism and solidarity are essential characteristics of postmodernism. My presentation of these characteristics has definitely been brief. However, it is sufficient for my purpose which is to describe the philosophical landscape in which I must locate my discussion on spirituality because philosophical concerns directly impact on concerns of spirituality.

William Johnston has argued that the philosophical changes that have taken place require that we move towards reconstruction (Johnston, 1987, pp.34-37). Thus, while broadly accepting many of the insights of postmodernism, in incorporating them into my conception of spirituality, I will attempt to develop a more positive approach than is common among postmodernist writers. My approach of reconstruction is similar to that taken by Griffin. Griffin has argued that postmodernism, which has mostly concerned itself with the deconstructive or eliminative task of critiquing contemporary life, must also be about a reconstructive or revisioning project as well. According to Griffin, a reconstructive approach would seek to formulate a postmodern worldview through a revisioning of modern premises and traditional concepts. Thus, a new unity of the scientific, ethical, aesthetic, and religious intuitions would be sought. Such a revisioning would seek to transcend modernity's emphasis upon individualism, anthropocentrism, patriarchy, mechanization, consumerism, rationalism, and militarism. A reconstructive postmodernism, in its synthesis of modern and premodern truths, would provide for an organicism and an acceptance of alternative ways of knowing to assist in finding our way through the challenges of our times. Griffin has argued that postmodernism must be future focused, communal, and welcoming of religious pluralism. He argues in favor of a transformative traditionalism, one that incorporates a religious spirituality as the only hope for positive social change (Griffin, 1988a, pp. x-xii). My thesis falls within a more reconstructive approach in that I seek to rework the traditional method of contemplation-in-action within our contemporary context.

Contemporary Challenges to Traditional Spirituality

Traditionally within Western culture spirituality has been associated with a person's relationship with a personal, transcendent being, often called God (Beck, 1990, p.159). However, today this traditional notion is being subjected to a much needed scrutiny from a populace that is more educated, more democratic, more individualistic, and more independent than perhaps ever before. Indeed, in our postmodern age we recognize a number of approaches that present legitimate challenges to traditional spirituality. These challenges come from several fronts, a few of which I summarize below.

i) Secular Humanism

Clive Beck has offered a clear presentation of the challenge which secular humanism has made to traditional spirituality. Beck opts for a concept of spirituality that distinguishes between a popular sense of religion, as might be found in a mainline church, and a broad sense of religion, as might be found in a person who would assent to mystery without necessarily assenting to a divinity.

> By spiritual, I mean possessing such qualities as awareness, integration, courage, love, and gentleness. Traditionally, spirituality (and religiousness) has often been tied to the notion of being in touch with and perhaps possessed by a divine being or order, but I am proposing a usage which would not require this as a component. (Beck, 1990, p.159)

Beck correctly argues that a person can be spiritual without being religious. He describes a spiritual person as aware, holistic, integrated, capable of wonder, grateful, hopeful, courageous, detached, loving, and gentle. Moreover, Beck argues that spirituality must be about both exteriority and interiority. That is, the concerns of the outer world, for taking care of oneself and one's loved ones, is integral to any spirituality. Finally, Beck suggests that religious and non-religious people need to overcome their mutual suspicion of each other and appreciate what the other has to offer with regard to spirituality (Beck, 1990, pp.163-166).

Beck responds to those who dismiss his position as mere secular humanism by arguing that those from religious worldviews can lay no claim to a monopoly on high ideals, depth, and moral living (Beck, 1990, pp.170-171). Beck is correct in this view for there are many who live a spiritual life without the support of a formal religion. More importantly, however, I think that Beck has articulated the foundations for recognizing spirituality in a secular and pluralist world. Such a recognition is sorely needed as more and more educational theorists who stand outside formal religions are pointing to the need to attend to the spiritual dimension of human life (Noddings, 1992, pp.81-85; Moffett, 1994, pp.5-32, 265-289; Plunkett, 1990, p. vii).

Beck challenges traditional spiritualities to move away from their tendency towards exclusion and superiority to a more inclusive attitude towards those outside their tradition (Beck, 1990, p.171). Spirituality, especially in Western societies, needs to be open to those who live spiritual lives within the secular and pluralist culture without the aid of religion. My book, in its attempt to be holistic and responsive to contemporary life, seeks to include the secular humanist position.

ii) Feminism

Traditional spiritualities, and in particular Western Christian spirituality, are also being challenged by feminism. The minimization of feminine figures in Christian scripture, the inclusion of mainly masculine images and titles of the divine, the organization of religious communities along patriarchal lines, the historical exclusion of women from ministerial leadership, and the presentation of spiritual growth as only linear rather than also cyclical are all aspects of a sexist legacy within Christianity. Keller has argued that the basic feminine sense of self is grounded in the world whereas the basic masculine sense of self is separated from the world (Keller, 1988, p.72). Taken to the extreme, this basic difference reinforces a dualism that results in disdain for the body, for women, and for the world. The result is a spirituality that prizes the mind over the body, male over female, and heaven over earth.

Feminist critique of traditional spiritualities has included a call for attention to the use of sexist and exclusive language and for the presentation of the divine in feminine images as well as masculine. Holland, Keller, and others have argued for a recovery of the feminine aspects of the divine and a recovery of the Goddess image (Holland, 1988, p.53; Keller, 1988, p.77). Historically within Christianity whenever the feminine side of spiritual life has been suppressed by patriarchy, the need to express a feminine spirituality has not disappeared but simply been redirected. One example of this redirection would be the Catholic movement 'from below' to call Mary, the mother of Jesus, the Mother of God, thus placing her on par with God. However, as Holland has argued (1988, pp.46-47), patriarchal religion responded to this threat to its authority by systematically marginalizing Mary from the center of Catholicism. The resulting incomplete presentation of the divine has been translated into an unhealthy spirituality that favors masculine values over feminine values.

Finally, some feminists advocate the end of patriarchal religion. Patriarchal religion is rooted in a belief in the superiority of the masculine image of God (Chittister, 1998, p.25). It leads to power over people, not power with people. It is a structural dynamic which is anti-women and anti-nature. Its foundation upon supernaturalism and transcendence without immanence is seen by many feminists as the root cause of much of the ecological devastation of our times. Finally, patriarchal religion when joined with a patriarchal society functions to oppress women.

> Patriarchy rests on four interlocking principles: dualism, hierarchy, domination, and essential inequality. These are the touchstones of the patriarchal worldview. These imply, in essence, that reason and feelings are distinct, that the world runs from the top down and that the top is genetically coded, that some humans are more human than other humans and so are in charge of them, that humans come in two sexes, one of which is fundamentally lesser than the other. Patriarchy takes biological differences, imposes hierarchy on them, gives hierarchy dominative power, and justifies all of it on the theory of intrinsic inequality. (Chittister, 1998, p.25)

Obviously, any spirituality that purports to be holistic and inclusive will have to deal intelligently with the challenges of feminism.

iii) Ecologism

Thomas Berry has argued that many of our current ecological problems can be traced to the effect of Christian spirituality upon our culture. Berry concerns himself more with public spirituality than with individual spirituality because he is concerned with the impact which spirituality has upon our social life. He argues that traditional Christian spirituality has helped to provide the context and has also supported the historical process whereby the human person has upset the ecological balance to such an extent that the survival of the planet is now in doubt (Berry, 1990, p.113).

Berry outlines four aspects of Christian spirituality that have contributed to the abuse of ecosystems. Christian spirituality has tended to see the divine as transcendent from the natural world and has viewed the natural world as a less than favorable place for the development of the divine and human relationship. Secondly, the continual insistence upon the end of the spiritual life being an eternal 'heaven' beyond this earth has weakened our appreciation and care of this natural home of ours. Thirdly, to some degree Christian spirituality adopted the mechanistic philosophy of modernity and sought to manipulate the natural world towards short-term gains without attention to the inner principles of life operative within the natural world. Finally, Berry argues that Christian spirituality has been tarnished by the Christian doctrine of a millennial age where peace, justice, and abundance will be attained as part of redemption through human actions directed towards this end. Berry contends that these aspects of Christian spirituality have been encoded within our culture and historical consciousness and, since the human community has acted from this consciousness, the result has been the devastation of the environment (Berry, 1990, pp.113-116). But, such action can no longer continue precisely because the earth can no longer bear it. A new consciousness is emerging wherein the effects of our philosophies and spiritualities on the natural world are painfully visible. This new consciousness calls for a new spirituality.

> Soon, however, we can expect a change. The imperatives of life and thought are too urgent for us to remain at the present impasse. As the Fathers of the church gave a new consciousness to Christianity through their association of Christian belief with Platonic philosophy, as Augustine and Dionysus gave a higher spiritual vision to Christianity through the insights of Neoplatonism, as Thomas gave new vigor to the Christian faith through his interpretation of Aristotle, so now a new vision and a new vigor are available to Christian tradition through our modern understanding of the origin and development of the universe and the emerging ecological age. If creating this new cultural coding of the ecological age is the next phase of the American experience, creating a spirituality integral with this coding may well be the next phase of the Christian tradition. (Berry, 1990, p.122).

Berry's proposal is that we must turn our attention to the earth, not the human person, as the primary location for meeting the divine. Turning our focus to the earth will result in a realignment of our concerns with the one true story upon which all humanity depends, the universe story. Thus, Berry, in his call for a 'functional cosmology' challenges traditional spiritualities to an entirely new and radical paradigm. This paradigm re-situates the human person back into his or her proper place within the cosmos. Undoubtedly, the turn to an ecological consciousness must be a major concern for spirituality today.

iv) Holism

Another recurring challenge to traditional spirituality is the call to move away from dualism to holism. Robert McAfee Brown has located the great fallacy of Western culture within a dualism that posits the following:

> sacred versus secular
> prayer versus politics
> faith versus works
> withdrawal versus engagement
> church versus world
> eternity versus time
> theory versus practice
> religion versus ethics
> soul versus body
> personal versus societal
>
> (Brown, 1988, p.27)

According to Brown, such dualism is the cause of the spiritual crisis facing our world. Some feminists would agree that the dualism of body and mind, matter and spirit, self and other, and world and deity (Keller, 1988, p.63), are the obstacles to a world where cooperation and connectedness are the norm not the exception. A rejection of dualism and materialism is essential to a postmodern spirituality (Griffin, 1988b, p.17).

Indeed, most authors who permit themselves to be called postmodern and who deal with the question of spirituality, agree that holism is a cornerstone to an appropriate and intelligent spirituality for our times. Berry has argued that for the first time in history all people are conscious of their connection to the single origin story of the universe. He argues that now is the time to establish a cultural coding that would promote the inter-connectivity of all living and nonliving components of the universe. For Berry, the individual is connected to all other beings (Berry, 1990, pp.120-122). Holland echoes this theme when he calls for an integrative approach that builds on the human person's oneness with nature (Holland, 1988, pp.52-54). That is, culture, institutions, and traditions must be seen as related to nature, otherwise a sustainable spirituality for the future is not possible.

Griffin has called this appeal to connection between ecological concern and human concern 'organicism.' He argues that the postmodern person feels at home in the world, not estranged from the natural world (Griffin, 1988a, p.ix). Keller too argues for holism, or interconnectedness, as the key to a new way. For her, the person is a self in relationship and this interconnectedness challenges the mechanistic and hierarchical mentalities of our time. She argues further that only in cooperation with feminism will post-modernists be able to move beyond the limits of dualism (Keller, 1988, pp.71-74).

This demand for an appreciation for holism, interconnectedness, and organicism not only has implications for our participation in the outer, objective world in which we operate. It also has implications for how we approach the inner subjective world of the person. That is, holism acknowledges the whole person: body, sense, sexuality, emotions, reason, intuition, imagination, and memory as well as the relationships through which the individual finds, creates, and sustains identity. Spirituality in light of holism must promote not only a holistic engagement in the world but also a holistic approach to the self.

In contemporary Western culture there is a diminishing role for traditional religions and an increasing tolerance for religious diversity. Our Western culture, driven by science and technology has tended to relegate the spiritual to the periphery in a way never before experienced. The patriarchy embedded in most religions is being exposed as leading to the oppression of women while the anthropocentric nature of religions, particularly Christianity, has been identified by some as a root for ecological devastation. The dualism of our world is being challenged by holism and an appeal to relatedness and interconnection. Finally, pluralism and diversity, which mark our age, are found within the various spiritualities that operate in our world.

The challenges to traditional spirituality described above need to be incorporated into any discussion regarding spirituality today. The critiques are valid and necessary and must be included within a reconstructive approach to spirituality. Doing this will result in a renewal of spirituality, one that will ultimately have transformative impact. Having discussed the postmodern landscape and summarized a few of the main challenges to traditional spirituality let us now turn to the area of education for spirituality itself.

Education and Spirituality

i) The Need for Spiritual Education

In light of the above reflections on contemporary challenges to traditional Western spiritualities the question of how to educate for a spiritual life in our times can be a little daunting. However, no matter how daunting, the need to educate for spirituality remains. Nel Noddings laments that there is so little attention to the spiritual life in education today (Noddings, 1992, p.49). She argues that spirit and body are joined and that consequently spirituality is too important to ignore. The movement towards an integrated self is assisted by the religious myths that "capture the spirit of people and encode its deepest fears, hopes, and longing" (Noddings, 1992, p.82). Noddings, much like Beck (1986, p.154), recognizes that spirituality must be the concern of both religious and non-religious people.

James Moffett argues that we need to elevate schooling itself to the spiritual level (Moffett, 1994, p. xiii). He sees this task as being independent of religion and centered on the goals of personal growth (Moffett, 1994, p.331). Moffett defines spirituality as follows:

> To be spiritual is to preserve our oneness with everybody and everything and to act on this perception. It is to be whole within oneself and with the world. (Moffett, 1994, p.xix)

Moffett, Noddings, Beck are representative of a school of educational thought that openly advocates the importance of educating for spirituality in our times. Indeed, Beck has argued that the word 'spirituality' itself needs to be retained and not substituted with other terms such as mental health, moral life, or maturity. Moreover, he argues that the term 'spirituality' can be a meeting point for both religious and non-religious persons.

> ... the word spirituality also has major advantages. It offers hope for a long overdue rapprochement between religious and nonreligious groups in this important task of education. It introduces an element of depth that has been lacking in discourse about public education. ... Furthermore, as noted earlier, the word spirituality and its cognates already have a strong foothold in ordinary, nonreligious language. In my opinion, it would be possible to gain acceptance for the word, the concept, and the goal in the realm of public education; and the

> advantages for such an acceptance would be considerable. (Beck, 1986, p.154)

I whole-heartedly agree with Beck's option for the term spirituality. I myself have explored using terms like 'inner life' and 'soul life' but have found these to be, while good, either too subjective or too restrictive. Moreover, I agree that the term spirituality forces all educators, whether religious or not, to grapple with a central feature of human life, the spiritual aspects. To use a less potent term would reduce the efficacy of any dialogue and consequent learning that might result when people from different walks of life try to handle the area of spirituality. As well, the current situation of our world demands an intelligent approach to spirituality if life on this planet is to advance.

I am in agreement with the school of educational theorists calling for education in spirituality. At the same time I am aware that paradoxically our contemporary culture, which so desperately needs such an education, is precisely that which makes such an education difficult to undertake. Indeed, some of the educational ideas operative today are impediments to educating for a holistic spirituality.

ii) Theoretical Obstacles to Educating for Spirituality

It is one thing to recognize the need for spirituality today and to argue for the importance of educating for it. It is quite another matter to actually embark on the task of such an education especially within a reconstructive framework. In particular when we turn to the area of formal education we can recognize that education itself is not really very conducive for fostering spirituality. Although our present education system is neither the only nor the best location to educate for spirituality it does provide a microcosm of the educational philosophy operative in our society. As such, entrenched within the formal education systems of our nation are some of the theoretical obstacles that lie in the way of educating for spirituality.

Contemporary education is overwhelmingly influenced by rationalism. Rationalism, one of the legacies of the Enlightenment, champions the role of reason in knowledge. Thus, knowledge which is valuable is knowledge that is reasonable and the competent person is the person who is capable of rational critique. In rationalism, cogitating takes precedence over all other ways of knowing.

When rationalism is followed as an educational philosophy we find that students are encouraged to 'think' and to develop critical thinking skills. Students learn content that can be memorized, categorized, applied, and tested by the teacher. The student is a knower who uses the mind to 'figure out' life. Hence, acquiring knowledge is often reduced to the acquisition of objective, empirical data that can be quantified and evaluated using rational reflection. Such knowledge is possessed mostly for its instrumental value and rarely for its intrinsic value. As Taylor argues, it is "instrumental reason" wherein "maximum efficiency, the best cost-output ratio, is its measure of success" (Taylor, 1991, p.5).

The teacher who follows rationalism is often concerned with the sophistication of thought shown by his/her students. What teacher doesn't delight in a student who can work with the subject matter with a high degree of synthesis and application skills? The value of the learning that takes place in a course is determined by the degree to which a student can use his/her reason to master the content. Understandably, tests and examinations become critical moments in the learning journey. This approach is epitomized by theories such as Bloom's taxonomy (Lorber and Pierce, 1983, pp.39-67).

Of course, our present educational approach is not purely so one-dimensional. There is an appreciation for the role of imagination and creativity in education (Egan,

1992, pp.45-65; Hare, 1993, pp.147-162), and these faculties are often ferreted out in the humanities or arts. Moreover, thanks to Dewey, there is an appreciation for the role of experience within learning, as is evident in such areas as experiments, group work, and subjective essays. However, these approaches are often merely tolerated or marginalized. At best their value lies in their usefulness in supporting the hegemony of instrumental rationalism. Regrettably, they are peripheral approaches that often run the risk of being eclipsed by rationalism.

Our world owes much to rationalism and it is not my intention to denigrate the role of reason in the pursuit of knowledge. Indeed, reason has propelled our civilization forward particularly through its influence in the areas of science and technology. The fruits of our scientific and technological culture abound everywhere. This is particularly true in our Western civilization. Now, there is nothing innately wrong with thinking for it is crucial to knowledge. However, when the thinking moment becomes the single overarching determining moment, then knowledge becomes one-dimensional. Thinking divorced from intuition, imagination, feeling, aesthetics, culture, values, and relationships often leads to knowledge that is incomplete. Such an approach leads people to know only partially, not wholly. It is as if people were asked to breathe with one lung when they were created with two.

Donald Oliver has taken up the critique of modern educational practice even further than the critique of rationalism. He argues that rationalism, science, and technology have resulted in a culture driven by the root metaphor of the machine (Oliver, 1989, p.19). The educational philosophy that serves this machine metaphor is that of technical knowing and its cherishing of functional specialization, hierarchy, and progressive specialization. The features of specialization and hierarchy are present not only within our formal education systems, with their emphasis upon specialized knowledge and a hierarchy of knowledge workers, but also throughout our entire social and economic culture.

Oliver argues that there are six themes to technical knowing. The first, rationality, focuses not so much on speculative reason as on pragmatic rationality so that everyday problems become the focus of learning. Second, componentiality is the belief that reality not only can be dissected into, but is constituted by, separate components. Thus, we divide learning into various subjects or departments, a move which feeds specialization. Oliver identifies multi-relationality as a third feature of technical knowing. Multi-relationality refers to the practice of seeing many factors as being necessary for technological production. Here, the machine metaphor is clearly visible, for just as a machine requires many parts to function, advances in technological production require many partners. This multi-relationality is apparent not only in the production of goods and services, including knowledge, but also in management practices that focus on partnerships, cooperatives, and stake-holders. Marketability, the fourth feature of technical knowing, is particularly noticeable in our day. In the present educational climate the focus is upon acquiring knowledge and skills that are directly translatable into employment. The fifth feature, that of plurality, is not one that values diversity so much as one that accentuates the distance between components or parties. Thus, in technical knowing there is a pluralism where differences not only never touch but can never enter into communication because the distance is too great. Finally, Oliver argues that modernity's focus on technical knowing as always progressive accentuates specialization in learning today (Oliver, 1989, pp.11-13).

For Oliver, the consequence of technical knowing is a fragmented view of reality and of life itself. From this type of knowledge we create functional and structured social systems that are often devoid of human relatedness. Thus, our education systems opt for promoting utilitarian and technical knowledge. The result is a diminished appreciation for imagination, for being in nature, for poetics in life. Ultimately, such a one-dimensional approach to knowledge results in a depleted sense of meaning and a diminished spiritual life. This is the result of not attending to the other dimension, the unity of being.

> Our assumption is that without some intuitive sense of their connections cultures and social systems lose their homeostatic balance between the separateness and the unity of being. The consequence of this loss is a mixture of arrogance, as we seek to dominate a nature that stands outside ourselves, and the loss of our inner spiritual will, as we lose the feeling for what it all means. (Oliver, 1989, p.58)

I agree with Oliver's description of the present obsession with technical and rational knowing. This approach to knowledge is deeply embedded within our culture, our education systems, and our individual and collective psyches. It has led to an over valuing of technical and practical knowledge within education as well as to education that promotes a fragmented view of life. This one-dimensional approach makes the task of educating for spirituality all the more difficult. The reason for this is that spirituality is concerned with connections, meaning, and relatedness. The present emphasis on technical and rational knowledge provides less than adequate conditions for educating for spirituality precisely because it is not concerned with seeking connections, promoting relationships, and discovering meaning. In order to move toward a more holistic approach, one that goes beyond the one-dimensionality of our present educational practice, we need to recover an appreciation for the ontological concerns of life. Such concerns are spiritual concerns. Education for spirituality today, then, must be engaged in with a dual awareness of both the need for spiritual life and the impediments to facilitating spiritual depth within contemporary educational practice.

iii) Defining Spirituality

Arriving at a common definition for spirituality is not easy. I agree with *Harper's Encyclopedia of Religious Education* when it says that "spirituality may be described but it is not readily defined, for the boundaries are broad" (Cully and Cully, 1971, p.607). Today it is very much the case that a comprehensive and universal definition of spirituality is not possible. Still, for the purposes of my book it is imperative that I enunciate, at least in some fashion, the field of concerns that the term spirituality needs to include today.

There are many differing definitions of spirituality. Indeed, David Griffin has posited that spirituality can mean many things to different people.

> For many people, the term spirituality has otherworldly connotations and implies some form of religious discipline. The term is used here in a broad sense, however, to refer to the ultimate values and meanings in terms of which we live, whether they be otherworldly or very worldly ones, and whether or not we consciously try to increase our commitment to those values and meanings. The term does have religious connotations, in that one's ultimate values and meanings reflect some presupposition as to what is holy, that is, of ultimate importance. But the presupposed holy can be something very worldly, such as power, sexual energy, or success. Spirituality in this broad sense is not an optional quality which we might elect not to have. Everyone embodies a spirituality, even if it be a nihilistic or materialistic spirituality. It is also, of course, customary to use spirituality in a stricter sense for a way of life oriented around an ultimate meaning and around values other than power, pleasure, and possession. (Griffin, 1988b, pp.1-2)

Griffin's definition is similar to Beck's broad definition of spirituality and has merit because of its appeal to people who would not consider themselves religious in a formal sense. Spirituality today must attend to our cultural context, part of which includes secular humanism, anti-authoritarianism, and anti-metanarratives. Any definition of spirituality must be broad enough to encompass all peoples and be respectful of pluralism. On the other hand, Griffin's definition tends towards a privatism and subjectivism in that the concern is more with defining spirituality as a personal matter. We must move beyond this limitation.

Thomas Berry has purposely opted for public spirituality because he sees the ecological devastation of our times as requiring us to break out of anthroprocentric spiritualities. "I am interested in public spirituality, which I describe as 'functional values and their means of attainment in an identifiable human community'" (Berry, 1990, p.110). For Berry the place of public life, via institutions, politics, and economics, is the essential arena for discussing spirituality. His departure, a radical one, permits him to turn towards the great concerns of economic justice (Berry, 1990, pp.70-88), sustainable development, and ecology and to posit a paradigm shift towards the universe story as the ultimate grounding spiritual experience for humankind (Berry, 1990, pp.123-137). Berry is correct in taking this direction and his thought breaks through the limits of traditional spiritualities.

Jim Wallis echoes Berry's pursuit of a public spirituality when he argues that spiritual values can contribute to a renewed vision of political life in North America.

> A new politics will require the spiritual resources of our best moral and religious traditions. More and more people, religious or not, are searching for a new spirituality as well as for a new politics. The two must be joined and proceed together. (Wallis, 1994, p.35)

Wallis, writing from an awareness of the bankruptcy of liberal and conservative politics and the divorce between politics and daily life, claims that only through a reconstruction of a spirituality as communal and political can ways be found to reverse the damage of social and economic decline (Wallis, 1994, pp.21-25). Both Berry and Wallis correctly call for a revival of spirituality that includes the public arenas of politics, economics, and ecology.

Spirituality today must be holistic. It must include the subjective experience of the person. It must include our body, our emotions, and our deepest longings. It must include the wider world around us, the demands of solidarity, and the story of the universe. It must take up the feminist challenge to be inclusive and concerned with grounding in relationship and interrelationship, between self and other, between selves and the world. It must take into account the global village we live in, a village marked by pluralism and diversity. It must include the public dimension and the areas of politics and economics. Finally, spirituality must be life affirming in promoting the deepest needs and aspirations for life that reside in the human person and which are connected to the global and ecological community.

I propose to define spirituality as the living from and acting out of awareness of the creative energy that flows from the "unbreakable bond of relatedness that makes the whole of the universe" (Berry, 1990, p.91). More specifically, the natural world to which the human person belongs is animated by a creative and dynamic energy. Plato called this energy the *anima mundi* or the soul of the world (Berry, 1990, p.22). This anima mundi unites that which is separate (O'Donoghue, 1997, p.118). This life giving energy forms the condition for personal individuation because "every being has its own interior, its self, its mystery, its numinous aspect" (Berry, 1990, p.134), which seeks expression in and through the world. The energy that comes from the relatedness that underlies the universe and from which life emerges is found in all of creation and within the human person. As such spirituality can be understood as the deliberate attentiveness to the life energy that sustains us personally and which grounds our social structures and the entire universe.

> The first principle is the primacy of spiritual energy. The foundation of all social energies – economic, political, and cultural – is spiritual. Spiritual energies and social forms constitute a single whole. Spiritual energies are the deepest source of the legitimation or transformation of society. (Holland, 1988, p.49)

Understood in this way, spirituality can be seen as a force for social transformation (Keller, 1988, p.76). This energy is found in the underlying unity and bond of relatedness found within the universe.

If spirituality is about living from the awareness of the energy that stems from the unity in the universe then it will require that we pursue a holistic and synergistic approach to life. The reason for this is that too often we live fragmented lives. Certainly in many areas of modern life we can notice the pull towards fragmentation. Now, life is complex and there is good in the multiplicity that characterizes daily life. However, too often fragmentation depletes our energy and undermines our living. The concern of spirituality, then, is to promote a harmonious and holistic lifestyle that is congruent with the fundamental unity that animates the universe. Understood in this way, spirituality is about living, not dogma or doctrine.

iv) Communion, Concord, and Incommensurability

There is a connectedness, a communion that grounds the universe. This underlying interrelatedness or unity of being can at times be apprehended, although not fully. This philosophical position, which favors a recovery of an ontological depth to life, is being advocated not only from the ecological prophets like Berry but within educational philosophy itself.

Oliver, writing in response to the fragmentation present within modern education, has called for a return to a grounded or ontological knowing to balance our postmodern fixation on technical knowing. In his view ontological knowing is a knowing that includes feelings, sensibilities, and thoughts that are moving, dynamic, and continually emergent. "With grounded or ontological knowing, we feel (usually unconsciously) the many aspects of an occasion evolve into the unity of event, as if out of nowhere" (Oliver, 1989, p.14). Central to Oliver's view of ontological knowing is the apprehension of connection to a larger world, a concern for the connection with being itself, and an awareness that ultimately "all is one" (Oliver, 1989, p.15).

Oliver's concern is to construct connections and bridges between fields rather than promoting progressive specialization of fields and fracturing. He calls for a return to an attention to religious sensibility of groundedness that is most often characterized by awe, reverence, and celebration of connectedness (Oliver, 1989, pp.53-54).

> The quality of religiosity in what we have called ontological knowing gives humans an experience of universal connectedness (with other forms of life, with nature, with the creative qualities of being and becoming, with the sense of oneness we often call God.) (Oliver, 1989, p.60)

This is the essential challenge for the modern world in Oliver's eyes. Without a return to a grounded ontology, the modern world will continue to fracture and splinter. The consequence will be a continual erosion of meaning and purpose.

Oliver argues that the process philosophy of Whitehead provides an appropriate method for pursuing a grounded ontology. Whitehead's process philosophy, with its emphasis on the integrity and interconnectedness of all being, promotes an appreciation for a oneness in life. This oneness or unity is found in the realm of being, God, soul, or mind, however one wants to call it (Oliver, 1989, p.103). Oliver is seeking to find a way to counteract the negative impacts of the machine metaphor by proposing the metaphor of an organism supported by grounded ontology and Whitehead's process. The focus then turns to that of being and becoming.

Oliver's appeal to ontology and to Whitehead's process philosophy corresponds to my position that we need to attend to the animating energy that permeates all of reality. His argument is similar to Berry's call for a recognition of the communion within the universe and the foundation of all life upon the principle of relatedness. This position is consistent with "the quintessential mystical insight" that the oneness of reality cuts across all cultures and religions (Lanzetta, 1996, p.91). Attention to the underlying connections and fundamental unity in life is foundational to developing a spiritual awareness and is a cornerstone to spiritual education.

Claiming a foundational communion, or a common ground to humanity, seems, at first glance, to contradict the insights regarding difference, culture, and community that permeates philosophical discourse today. Boyd has warned that the appeal to unity simply falls into the trap of universalism which "can dictate a prescriptive denial of diversity" (Boyd, 1996, p.622). Boyd rejects any tendency towards universalism because, in his view, it leads those who hold such views to try to dominate others (Boyd, 1996, p.627). There is some merit to this position. Indeed, as Taylor, has pointed out, modernity emerged precisely by the breaking free of the constraints of universalisms (Taylor, 1991, p.3). This was a necessary historical development. As a result of this break from universalism contemporary culture is marked by difference and incommensurability and has moved far away from the notions of unity and common ground.

Still I believe we can affirm an underlying relatedness or fundamental unity to the universe while also affirming difference and incommensurability. It is true that "one of the lovely things about us as individuals is the incommensurable in us. In each person, there is a point of absolute nonconnnection with everything else and with everyone" (O'Donoghue, 1997, p.98). According to Berry this is due to the fact that beyond the fundamental principle of relatedness that grounds the universe story there is the second principle that drives the universe and this is the principle of differentiation. The primordial energy of the universe seeks ongoingly to create and express itself. When expressed through human subjectivity we have culture, difference, and history (Berry, 1990, p.106). Hence, we need to simultaneously affirm both communion and incommensurability. Keller agrees with Berry that oneness doesn't negate the differences of the many for "in the 'theatre of interrelations', spirituality – for men as well as women – can only mean centering by connecting, and connecting by centering" (Keller, 1988, p.78).

Panikkar, who has been called "a maverick or gadfly pluralist" (Knitter, 1996, p.178), has made inroads in such a dual affirmation. On the one hand Panikkar affirms that the fundamental fact of life is that every being is constituted by relationship with other beings. Like Berry, it is the grounding in the web of relationships which forms the unity that in turn permits diversity.

> Every being is what it is precisely because it is itself an ensemble of relationships and enters into intimate, constitutive relationship with other beings. And this relationship is such that it forms a radical unity

> that does not render things uniform, but, on the contrary, permits
> them to be diverse. Unity, then, and not the contrary, is the
> fundamental fact. (Panikkar quoted in Lanzetta, 1996, pp.91-92)

Such an understanding leads Panikkar to be able to affirm "the inherent pluralism of
reality, which is, at the same time, one" (Lanzetta, 1996, p.96).

Panikkar is able to make such a claim because he distinguishes pluralism
from plurality and pluriformity. According to Panikkar, pluralism stands upon the
recognition that no one system of thought is complete in itself. In pluralism one
recognizes 'the legitimate coexistence of systems of thought, life, and action which,
on the other hand, are judged incompatible among themselves" (Panikkar, 1995,
p.34). Plurality and pluriformity however rest on the misguided assumption that one
system can provide a complete, universal interpretive framework that can be
concretized in many ways (Panikkar, 1995, pp.42-43). An example of plurality
would be the various ways of being a Christian. An example of pluralism would be
the major world religions which, despite sharing some common ground, are radically
different. Pluralism requires a positive acceptance of diversity and a resistance to
any tendency to artificially unite what is definitively different. Pluralism, which is
quite distinct from plurality, sees differences as varied manifestations of unity and
incommensurate with any monolithic unity which would negate differences.

> Pluralism stands between unrelated plurality and a monolithic unity.
> It implies that the human condition in the present reality should not
> be neglected, let alone despised in favor of an ideal (?) situation of
> human uniformity. One the contrary, it takes our factual situation as
> real and affirms that in the actual polarities of our human existence
> we find our real being. (Panikkar, 1978, pp. xxvii-xxviii)

Such a position permits Panikkar to accept that there are many absolutes and many
truths that cannot be reduced to 'one' universal absolute or truth. Panikkar, then,

affirms both pluralism and unity by arguing that unity is the condition for pluralism while true pluralism is incommensurate with unity (Knitter, 1996, p.180).

Hence, unity does not negate diversity. Moreover, to deny diversity would be to deny freedom (Coward, 1995, p.47), and the creative impulse operative in the universe. There exists a creative tension between the drive for differentiation that results in diversity and the existence of a fundamental communion. We need to accept this tension for within this tension, creativity is found. Finally, pluralism enhances spiritual life for "spiritual growth arises not from religious isolationism, but rather in the context of religious pluralism" (Coward, 1995, p.62).

Panikkar argues that we can live in this tension if we accept the need for concord in life. That is, embracing pluralism as the necessary dynamic of life need not necessitate the negation of unity if we accept the need for consensus. "Consensus ultimately means to walk in the same direction not to have just one rational view" (Knitter, 1996, pp.182-183). For Panikkar, a sense of concord, or harmony, emerges when we seek a consensus in moving toward the oneness in life without ceasing to be different or trying to become one (Knitter, 1996, p.182). From within concord, the creative tension between pluralism and unity can be sustained, accepted and lived. Communion and unity can co-exist with pluralism and incommensurability.

Contemplation and Action

i) A Traditional Spirituality

Most religions of the world have traditionally upheld that the human person is constituted by both a contemplative and active dimension. In fact, contemplation and action was the topic of a unique conference held in Texas in 1977. At that conference representatives from Judaism, Christianity, Native America, Buddhism, Islam, and Sufism discussed the traditional approaches to contemplation and action in light of the modern world (Ibish and Wilson, 1977). Despite differences, a constant in the dialogue was the appreciation for attentiveness to the underlying unity of life and acting in accordance with this awareness.

Within the Christian tradition there has been a long-standing appreciation for the contemplative life as a life devoted to developing attention to the underlying unity that permeates life. Although it has been recognized that the contemplative life needs to be lived in conjunction with the active life of service, the contemplative life has often been viewed as superior to the active within traditional Christianity. This was particularly true during the monastic period when the contemplation of transcendent, otherworldly, divine truths took precedence over the concerns of the world. There was a fair degree of dualistic stoicism in all this.

With the dawning of the modern age a notable shift in contemplative spirituality took place. The active life took on as much importance as the contemplative life. Chittister has pointed out that the greatest contemplatives were often the most active people (Chittister, 1998, p.2). The lives of Teresa of Avila, John of the Cross, Catherine of Sienna and the Rhineland mystics bear witness to this development.

The person who succeeded in bringing the contemplative tradition into the modern world was Ignatius of Loyola (Gutierrez, 1985, p.26). From his own life experience, in which he struggled to live a contemplative life within his historical context, Ignatius of Loyola provided a creative solution to the problem of contemplation and/or action. Ignatius recognized that there are times when we are invited to spend time in nurturing our souls, our inner life, through contemplative practices and that there are times when we need to devote ourselves to the activities necessary to sustain our lives. He was also very aware that the modern world presented particular challenges to living a spiritual life.

The broadening of the known world by geographical discoveries, the assertion of human reason that found expression in the birth of experimental science, the extension of the scope of human subjectivity in religious matters as evidenced by the Protestant Reformation – these were converging phenomena that led to a new way of understanding the role of human freedom. It was not a mere coincidence that freedom, a freedom directed to the service of God and others, should be a central theme in Ignatian spirituality. (Gutierrez, 1985, p.27)

Ignatius advocated contemplation-in-action and wrote the now famous Ignatian Exercises to assist people to become contemplatives-in-action. Through the practice of the Exercises Ignatius believed that the divorce between the active and contemplative dimensions could be overcome. He proposed that the ideal was to contemplate while one was active and to bring one's active life into one's contemplation. Thus, he proposed a method for 'contemplation-in-action', which was an appropriate response for his times (O'Callaghan, 1974, pp.13-14).

ii) Contemplation and Liberating Praxis: A Credible Option

The tension between the active and the contemplative life continues in our time and the direction, which St. Ignatius offered, can provide some insights into how to live a spiritual life today. Indeed, contemplation-in-action can be a credible spirituality for our day. However, before we can embrace this method we need to broaden our understanding of the contemplative and active dimensions and how these two dimensions function today.

We need to understand the contemplative dimension as involving attentiveness to the interconnections in all of creation that stem from the unity of being. Moreover, we must understand contemplation as seeking the life energy that flows from this fundamental unity, a unity which in no way negates difference but rather grounds pluralism. In fact, it is precisely the unity within creation that provides the energy for differentiation and the resulting pluralism. Contemplation is consistent with the call of feminists and ecologists for attention to the centrality of relatedness and interconnection. It is consistent with the need to move beyond dualism toward holism and organicism. Finally, the contemplative's attention to connectedness and unity, which is an appeal to ontological knowing, can be embraced by secular humanists for it does not necessarily require an assent to a divine being or God.

Our understanding of the active dimension must also reflect our historical context. Hence, we need to attend to the demands of solidarity as a constitutive ingredient for justice. We must understand the human person as a creative agent of change rather than an object of history. We need to include the principles of democracy and equality as cornerstones to Western culture. We need to consider the impact of social and political structures on our living conditions. As such, we need to include the economy, politics, culture, and the environment within our understanding of the active life. The active dimension requires an appreciation of the need for liberating praxis as a necessary constitutive element of spirituality. Liberating praxis is necessary in order to widen our understanding of the active life so as to include the social and political areas of life.

Clive Beck has described a spiritual person as possessing awareness, integration, courage, love, gentleness, hope, gratitude, acceptance, detachment, and a capacity for wonder (Beck, 1990, p.159). In doing so, he has expressed some of the goals of the spiritual life. My concern is with how to educate for a spiritual life. As such, my topic is concerned more with articulating a method for spiritual education than with the goals of spiritual life, although I do not discount the importance of the goals.

In light of this, I propose that contemplation and liberating praxis are best pursued within a dialectical relationship. This dialectic will create the conditions and the possibilities for a much-needed holism in spirituality. The dialectical process between contemplation and engagement in liberating praxis must eventually become so fluid that the Ignatian ideal of contemplation-in-action becomes a model for our times. Thus, one contemplates while engaged in works of liberation and solidarity and one brings their experience of engagement in praxis to their contemplation. The resulting 'contemplation-in-liberating praxis' would provide a method for growing in the spiritual life today.

Conclusion

I have tried to situate my concern with how to educate for contemplation-in-action within our historical context. The world we live in and seek to educate in is varied and complex. Moreover, the field of education itself, imbedded as it is in approaches that promote fragmentation and techno-rationality, is limited in terms of viable methods for educating for spirituality. Despite the limitations, there is a tremendous need to educate for a spiritual life.

The method for spiritual education that I am proposing falls within a reconstructive postmodernism that seeks to integrate tradition within a holism or organicism that respects pluralism and diversity. My appeal to a reframing of contemplation-in-action as contemplation-in-liberating praxis can be supported philosophically by retrieving our appreciation for ontology. It is my belief that an appeal to ontology can be a meeting point for those who espouse secular humanism, feminism, ecologism, holism, and pluralism. It is also my belief that we must broaden our understanding of the active life to include the social, economic, and political areas of human life. Including these areas requires an appreciation of them as valid locations for engaging in spiritual action. Building upon these foundations, contemplation-in-liberating praxis can be a credible method for spiritual education today.

My concern in this chapter has been to address some of the more theoretical issues affecting my theory. I now need to draw out more completely what is meant by 'contemplation-in-liberating praxis'. The first step is to discuss the contemplative dimension which is the task of the next chapter.

CHAPTER TWO

CONTEMPLATION AS WONDERSTRUCK BEHOLDING

Then one day I was walking along Tinker Creek thinking of nothing
at all and I saw the tree with the lights in it. I saw the backyard cedar
where the mourning doves roost charged and transfigured, each cell
buzzing with flame. I stood on the grass with the lights in it, grass
that was wholly fire, utterly focused and utterly dreamed. It was less
like seeing than like being for the first time seen, knocked breathless
by a powerful glance. The flood of fire abated, but I'm still spending
the power. ... I have since only very rarely seen the tree with the lights
in it. The vision comes and goes, mostly goes, but I live for it....
(Dillard, 1988, pp.33-34)

In the midst of the contemporary challenges to traditional Western spirituality

outlined previously there is a growing appreciation within both secular and religious

educational circles of the need for a renewed approach to spiritual education. While

there are significant philosophical impediments to educating for spirituality within

Western culture there remains some hope in revisioning education for a spiritual life

if we can broaden our scope and understanding of spirituality. We need to move

towards an understanding of spirituality as attentiveness to the creative energy that

is rooted in the fundamental relatedness and unity that forms the universe. At the

same time we need to include within our understanding of spirituality the need for

active engagement in the social realm. The traditional spiritual method of

contemplation-in-action, if broadened to incorporate our contemporary

consciousness, can be a credible spirituality for our times. It can be an appropriate spiritual method if we understand contemplation as attention to oneness, connection, and communion and action as including social and political action.

The goal of this chapter is to discuss how we can understand the contemplative dimension of human life today. I will begin with a discussion of what is meant by contemplation. This will be followed by a discussion of how mysticism and contemplation can be seen as a fundamental human spirituality. After this I will discuss how contemplation provides a way to move beyond the limits of techno-rationalism and disconnected abstraction both of which permeate Western culture and education. I will then argue that contemplation is compatible with a holistic educational philosophy. Finally, the relationship between the active and the contemplative dimensions of human life will be described as a prelude to the following chapter which will be devoted entirely to the question of action for liberating praxis.

Contemplation as Wonderstruck Beholding

Margret Buchmann has argued that contemplation is "a wonderstruck thinking that is neither willing nor scientific knowing" (Buchmann, 1989, p.36). It requires that one suspend their willing forms of inquiry and seek to perceive events, people, and things just as they are. Buchmann is careful not to discount the use of the intellect in her understanding of contemplation. What she argues is that contemplation happens when a person arrives at a point where their intellectual activity is brought to a rest and when they are content to simply 'behold' reality in its fullness.

> The contemplative life may involve a kind of application in cogitation or mediation. But contemplation is the point where activity comes to rest: its essential qualities are those of wonderstruck beholding, as we

attend to some desirable or lovable good – especially any truth
whatever – and dwell on it. This requires clarity of vision and serenity
in a quiet kind of looking. (Buchmann, 1989, p.49)

Understood in this way, contemplation can be defined as wonderstruck beholding of

the world. The entire universe can be contemplated.

Elsewhere, contemplation has been described as taking a "long loving look

at the real" (Burghardt, 1984, p.8). Here contemplation is understood as seeing

reality as it is and looking at reality with loving eyes. I would contend that

contemplation includes wonderstruck beholding and loving attention and also an

experience of being awakened to the life giving energy that exists in the universe.

A person who contemplates is "attentive to the radiance of each moment" (Panikkar,

1981, p.267). In beholding such radiance one is filled with wonder, awe, and energy.

Like Annie Dillard, quoted above, contemplatives find energy in beholding the

universe and are sustained in their living through such energy.

Contemplation is primarily an experiential way of knowing. Hence, when

one contemplates one strives not for knowledge through abstraction or objectification

but through subjective experiences of reality gained while being intentionally

attentive to reality. Contemplation is essentially a way of seeing, a way of

perceiving, and a way of beholding. Panikkar has called this way an 'attitude' that

involves mindfulness, awareness, enlightenment, and concentration (Panikkar, 1981,

p.261).

This way of beholding is not without a purpose for in contemplation one

seeks the "hidden centrum" (Panikkar, 1981, p.261), that grounds the universe. This

seeking is an action of the person who seeks to grow in the awareness of the

underlying unity that permeates the universe. Understood in this way, contemplation

is not a withdrawal from the world into introspection (Buchmann, 1989, p.47).

Rather, contemplation requires an outward focus in which one seeks to behold the life-giving communion in the universe. A contemplative is aware of the diversity that characterizes the universe but acknowledges that such diversity is a natural consequence of the creative energy that is found in the unity of the universe itself. What a contemplative seeks is to maintain an awareness of the fundamental unity that grounds all of reality, not so as to promote uniformity but rather to uphold the source of diversity. Contemplation, then, with its outward focus is a form of mysticism as unifying vision.

> In contrast, mysticism as unifying vision (exemplified by Eckhart) "knows nothing of inwardness." In this vision, the multiplicity of the world is transcended in an intuition of the fundamental unity, not simply of the world, but of the transcendent One itself. (Price, 1987, p.182)

Contemplation involves a deliberate attempt to seek the interconnections and the unity that exists beyond all the differences in the universe.

Contemplation is often accompanied by a sense of awe and reverence for life. It causes an amplification of awareness of the "benignity at the heart of the universe, the sense of meaning, the ultimate graciousness of life" (Dyckman and Caroll, 1981, p.79). Such awareness leads to wonder and to a sense of gratitude. Moreover, contemplation leads to playfulness, fuels creativity, and helps one feel at 'home' in the universe.

When one contemplates one needs to let go of prescriptions, preconceptions, and prejudices so as to be open to, surprised by, and moved by the real world. Otherwise we "see only what we want to see or what our perceptual and cognitive structures let us see" (Barry and Connolly, 1982, p.51). Contemplation requires a radical openness so as to be able to see reality clearly. Such openness and receptivity is heightened when one is relaxed. Annie Dillard puts it quite nicely when she says,

> But there is another kind of seeing that involves a letting go. When I see this way I sway transfixed and emptied. The difference between the two ways of seeing is the difference between walking with and without a camera. When I walk with a camera I walk from shot to shot, reading the light on a calibrated meter. When I walk without a camera, my own shutter opens, and the moment's light prints on my own silver gut. When I see this second way, I am above all an unscrupulous observer. (Dillard, 1988, p.31)

Walking with a sense of openness and expectancy, a person is better able to behold the wonders and beauties of life than if one rushed into reality with hard, preconceived notions of how reality 'ought to be'. The contemplative stance is one of openness, listening, and receptivity. It requires an attitude of openness and awareness much akin to Dillard's walking with her own shutters open.

While contemplation, understood as wonderstruck beholding of the fundamental unity in the universe, cannot be limited to rational or conceptual knowledge, it normally includes such knowledge. At the same time, contemplation cannot be reduced to only a matter of rational perception. No, contemplation, because it includes an experiential and intuitive awareness of reality as one, involves the whole person in their knowing.

Some philosophers try to explain this type of knowing as 'connatural'. The term 'connatural' knowledge has been used to describe the type of knowledge a person has when they are 'at-one-with' the reality around them. An example of this type of knowledge can be found in two people who are in love. They may be able to explain conceptually their reasons for being in love, but the knowledge that they are actually in love is an experiential one. They share this knowledge in their bodies, their emotions, and their intuitions. Their experience of intimacy and oneness does not mean that they lose their individuality. Quite the contrary, for the 'at-one-with', the being 'at home with', the other provides a necessary condition for the growth of the individual. A couple's experience of love as being 'at-one-with' the other is an example of connatural knowing (Russell, 1987, p.196). The term connatural is synonymous with the term contemplation for they both point to the apprehension of knowledge that is unifying and real.

Thomas Merton, the writer monk, expressed the importance of contemplation in the following way.

> Contemplation is the highest expression of man's intellectual and spiritual life. It is that life itself, fully awake, fully active, fully aware that is alive. It is spiritual wonder. It is spontaneous awe at the sacredness of life, of being. It is gratitude for life, for awareness, and of being. (Merton, 1967, p.1)

Contemplation is, as Merton says, the pinnacle of both intellectual and spiritual knowing. It is true that we come to learn of the world around us through our senses. It is also true that we learn through the use of reason for it is our capacity to reason which makes us conscious. These ways of knowing are part of contemplation for both senses and reason are involved when we seek to 'look lovingly at the real'. However, contemplation complements and supplements the knowledge gleamed from our senses and our reason by including experiential knowledge of the unity that grounds our living. Finally, contemplative knowledge provides an energy and an understanding of connections that both permits and requires a holistic approach to knowing.

As a way of knowing, contemplation presumes a way of being in the world that stands upon a belief that life and reality are grounded in an often hidden unity.

Some call this unity the Source, Being, the Tao, the Soul, the Collective Unconscious, the implicate order, etc. (Miller, 1994, p.3). Many would not even place a name on this reality. Yet, regardless of the nomenclature, the contemplative is one who continually beholds and wonders at the underlying oneness of the universe.

Mysticism and Contemplation

William James, in his famous work *The Varieties of Religious Experience*, presents an apt description of mysticism. According to him mystical experiences are experiences of oneness with the Absolute, or ground of being, and are ineffable, noetic, transitory, and passive (James, 1961, pp.299-300).

> This overcoming of all the usual barriers between the individual and the Absolute is the great mystic achievement. In mystic states we both become one with the Absolute and we become aware of our oneness." (James, 1961, p.323)

James argues further that such experiences are grounding for those who have them and provide a force, or in Dillard's words, an energy, from which to live. However, despite the conviction which such experiences might give to one, James argues that mystics have no right to demand from those who haven't had such an experience an assent to the authority of the experience (James, 1961, p.333). On the other hand, James argues that the fact that some people do have such experiences does call into question the pretension that non-mystical knowledge is the only form of knowledge (James, 1961, p.335).

I refer here to James' description of mystical experience and to Dillard's experience of the 'tree with the lights in it' in order to clarify my understanding and use of the terms mystic and contemplative. In my view, a mystic is one who beholds the oneness of reality and who discovers in this beholding an energy that fuels life. However, as James' argues, such experiences of beholding are transitory. 'The vision comes and goes', as Dillard states.

Although most religious traditions uphold a mystical tradition, mystical experience is not reserved for those who fall within a religious tradition. Dag Hammarskjold is a fine example of a mystic who stood outside formal religion and who sought to integrate within his personal and professional life the active and mystical dimensions of life (Hammarskjold, 1964, p.23). Moreover, many scientists attest to the importance of the mystical experience. For example, Palmer relates how Barbara McClintok, the winner of the Nobel Prize in science, was eulogized as "a mystic who knew where the mysteries lie but who did not mystify" (Palmer, 1997, p.11). Because of its availability to religious and non-religious persons we can say that the experience of the mystical is a primal human experience.

A mystic, in my view, is one who 'knows where the mystery lies but who does not mystify'. I think that too great an emphasis has been placed upon the ineffable nature of primal mystical experience, the result being that either people dismiss the claims of those who have such experiences or people who have such experiences fail to recognize their experiences as mystical. John Fenton has argued that too great a barrier has been placed between mystical experience and its interpretation (Fenton, 1995, p.189). This has led to a certain elitism in religious knowledge. Fenton argues that the incommunicability of mystical experience is not quite as strong as some would contend.

> A certain degree of indescribability or ineffability therefore seems characteristic of mystical experience. But if there are comparable experiences and if these are analogues to mystical experience in

common human experience then even for the nonmystic the
ineffability of language about mystical experience cannot be absolute.
Mystical ineffability is weak rather than strong. (Fenton, 1995,
p.193)

I think that Fenton's argument has merit for it permits a demystification of mysticism
and allows for locating mystical experience within the realm of common experience
available to anyone.

Dyckman and Caroll point out that many common experiences are in fact
mystical.

We all have "mystic" experiences. We are moved, momentarily at
least, by the absolute loneliness of a mountain peak, or the sun setting
over the ocean, or the incredible gift of friendship. We are awed at
the loveliness of a child, a poem, a painting. ...We exist in different
frameworks, theologies, lifestyles, language sets, but all, it seems to
us, are invited into such experiences. All are called to be mystics.
(Dyckman and Carroll, 1981, pp.79-80)

A mystic or a contemplative is one who, having been wonderstruck in their
beholding, continually looks for this experience again. The stance of continually
looking is the contemplative stance, wherein one strives to let reality reveal itself in
all its fullness. Reality, in both its differentiation and its foundational unity, yields
an energy that grounds life. A contemplative is one who seeks to behold the real
world and to wonder at both the unity, and difference, operative in reality.

The contemplative experience of wonderstruck beholding of oneness is not
dependent upon books, doctrine, or ordination. Rather, this experience can happen
anywhere and is available to any person precisely because they are human.
Understandably, because of its availability to all who are human, it is a spirituality
that does not augur well with institutional religions. "Today, as in the twelfth century

days of St. Francis of Assisi, mystics are not immediately popular with the institutional church because they are difficult to control, are fervently independent, and therefore subjects of suspicion" (Chrisci, 1986, p. iii). Moreover, where religious institutions seek to give structure to religious experience mysticism operates in an unstructured fashion, an approach that ultimately clashes with hierarchical institutions.

> Mysticism can occur, then, in all religions; and it almost always clashes head-on with the hierarchy dominant in its time. It is an experience of God, an experience of being one with God, an experience that God bestows on people. It is a call that people hear or perceive, an experience that breaks through the existing limitations of human comprehension, feeling, and reflection. ... The crucial point here is that in the mystical understanding of God, experience is more important than doctrine, the inner light more important than church authority, the certainty of God and communication with him more important than believing in his existence or positing his existence rationally. (Soelle, 1984, pp.86-87)

Mystical experience is not some exclusive way that is reserved for a select few. Indeed, contemplation is open to all regardless of culture, race, class, gender, or religion. "It makes no difference... whether these experiences are interpreted with the aid of a personal God or non-theistically, as in oriental mysticism" (Soelle, 1984, p.89).

This is a point that I wish to emphasize. The mystical experience is open to everyone by virtue of his or her humanity. People do have experiences where they behold the fundamental unity within the universe and where they come away with a sense of wonder and awe at life. Sometimes they recognize a deity in these experiences. Sometimes they do not. My work as a chaplain confirms that such experiences are more common than we think. The teacher who tells me that she had an experience of the wonder of creation when looking into the eye of a whale one summer; the student who tells me that ever since she felt a 'woosh' through her body her confusion around religion vanished; the nurse who speaks of a moment of being transfixed for a time while in New York City and how her life changed afterwards; and the mother who tells me that stroking her son while he sleeps is the deepest experience of communion with life for her; all speak of a mystical experience. Those who have such experiences do not always have the 'language' or the meaning system to explain or support the experience, but they have what Dillard would call an 'energy' which can in turn fuel their life with meaning and purpose.

We hear so little about mystical experiences not because they don't happen but because we have such little language to express these experiences. Religious language and symbolism, music, and poetics point to these experiences but certainly do not exhaust the description of them. The problem that arises with this non-communication is that these experiences, when not communicated, tend to be lost (Soelle, 1984, p.89). The result is that this fundamental spirituality is difficult to encourage, sustain, or teach (Merton, 1967, p.5; Panikkar, 1981, p.271).

From here on I shall opt for the term 'contemplative' rather than mystic for three reasons. First, despite the naturalness of such experiences, I recognize that many people mistrust the term mysticism because it carries with it too negative a connotation. This is due to the too often severe asceticism associated with mysticism in traditional religions and to the often over-emphasis upon the ineffability of mystical experience. Second, many people do have experiences of beholding the underlying oneness in the universe that consequently changes their consciousness and yet do not necessarily see this as either distancing them from ordinary life or requiring that they align themselves with a formal religious tradition. Third, I opt for the term contemplative because many people, even if they have not beheld the underlying unity in the universe, do respond to the claim that such experiences are possible and do naturally contemplate with the sometimes unconscious intention of apprehending the unity which mystics claim exists. For my purposes the term contemplation captures sufficiently the direction I wish to take, which is to behold the interconnections and unity that exists in the universe. A contemplative, then, regardless of whether or not they have had a mystical experience and regardless of whether or not they belong to a specific religion, is one who seeks to behold the underlying unity in the universe and seeks to live from the energy that such discovery can yield.

Contemplation, Technical Rationality, and Education

Previously I discussed the views of Donald Oliver on the present state of education and the impact of technical rationality on education. Despite the good in technical rationality, the result has been an entrenchment of a fragmented view of reality and life in modern consciousness. Such fragmentation has inhibited our capacity to learn in an organic and holistic fashion. It has also tended to undermine and deplete the energy needed to address contemporary life in a healthy and holistic fashion.

Daly and Cobb have described how such fragmentation has impacted upon academic learning. Recalling Whitehead's notion of "the fallacy of misplaced concreteness" where thinkers forget how far their abstractions have removed them from actual reality (Daly and Cobb, 1994, p.36), they locate the central flaw in contemporary higher education in unrooted abstractions. Such a flaw has resulted in the idolatry of academic disciplines wherein methods that promote excessive abstractions are vigorously pursued much to the detriment of an interdisciplinary and organic approach that is needed today in order to promote human well-being (Daly and Cobb, 1994, pp.123-126).

Thomas Merton also recognized the danger of excessive abstraction and he argued that this could be located in the Cartesian "cogito ergo sum".

> Nothing could be more alien to contemplation than the cogito ergo sum of Descartes. "I think, therefore I am." This is the declaration of an alienated being, in exile from his own spiritual depth, compelled to seek some comfort in a proof for his own existence. If his thought is necessary as a medium through which he arrives at the concept of his existence, then he is in fact moving further away from his true being. He is reducing himself to a concept. He is making it impossible for himself to experience, directly and immediately, the mystery of his own being. ... For the contemplative, there is no cogito ("I think."), and no ergo ("therefore"), but only sum, I am. (Merton, 1967, p.7)

Merton has correctly identified as problematic our contemporary tendency to engage in excessive abstractions that are alienated from real life. Such a tendency simply adds to the fragmentation of our understanding of the world and ultimately contributes to dehumanization.

What we need today is to return the use of reason to its proper place within human knowing. A contemplative approach to life seeks to do this. Unlike the Cartesian starting point of 'thinking', the starting point for the contemplative way is attentiveness to 'being'. That is, contemplative knowledge begins with the ontological, the experience of being in the world and moves to the rational as a secondary step. The primary step is the attentiveness to being. Unlike Merton who would argue for pure 'sum', I suggest that 'Sum, ergo cogito' (I am, therefore, I think.) more accurately reflects the contemplative way of knowing which includes our intellect.

Contemplation does not permit dislocated abstraction or the pursuit of knowledge divorced from reality. A true contemplative neither seeks to withdraw into abstractions in his/her mind or to avoid difficulties in the real world. On the contrary, contemplation requires the directing of one's attention to being in the real world and avoiding disconnected abstractions.

> The true contemplative is not less interested than others in normal life, not less concerned with what goes on in the world, but more interested, more concerned. ... The thing that distinguishes him from other men ... is that he has a much more spiritual grasp of what is "real" and what is "actual". (Shannon, 1981, p.139)

Contemplation, then, requires that we move beyond the fragmentation and "disciplinolatry" (Daly and Cobb, 1994, p.125) that presently characterizes education. It requires that we begin to work, teach, and think in ways that are rooted in a holistic appreciation of reality.

In my view the contemplative attentiveness to the experience of being creates the possibility for a more holistic approach to knowing. If I attend to my experience of being a person located in this real world then I have to admit that I learn in a variety of ways and that my thinking is only one way. As a human being I come to know through my emotions, intuitions, senses, premonitions, hunches, friendships, actions, experiences, imagination, beliefs, and dreams. Each of these is a door to knowledge. These ways of learning challenge the hegemony of the scientific, technical, and rational approaches. Moreover, if included within education they can help counteract unhealthy abstractions and rationalism.

Contemplation challenges us to attend to the fullness of life and to be open to being wonderstruck by the awesome energy that permeates the universe. The contemplative stance challenges the predominant scientific and technological view of education by pointing to the underlying unity that grounds our world.

> The structure of reality is not exhausted by the principles of empiricism and rationality. Reality's ultimate structure is that of an organic, interrelated, mutually responsive community of being. (Palmer, 1983, p.53)

A contemplative, in seeking to behold this community of being, ultimately tries to bring to education a concern for wisdom (Merton, 1968, p.224), rather than for the accumulation of knowledge.

Contemplation and Holistic Education

Parker Palmer has argued that we need "wholesight" in education (Palmer, 1983, p. xi). Palmer rejects the objectivism that permeates all of Western education arguing that it has contributed to a lack of depth and spirit in our times. For Palmer, a person knows not only through their senses and reason, but also through their intuitions, beliefs, emotions, actions, body, and relationships. He argues that we need to include all ways of knowing so as to be truly 'whole'. From such a holism, Parker argues we can achieve personal wholeness and then act to heal the world around us.

Palmer's concern has been with the area of spiritual education. Yet, others have echoed his call for "wholesight". Indeed, there is an emerging field within educational theory and practice that is called holistic education. Jack Miller has been a leader in this area.

In *The Holistic Teacher*, Miller argues that holism is concerned with discovering the interconnections that exist in life.

> A central principle underlying all of this is an awakening to the interconnectedness of all life. This same sense of interconnectedness is central to holistic education. (Miller, 1993, p.4)

Holistic education involves balancing the different poles that are found in life (male-female; outer-inner; rational-intuitive; material-sacred; etc.). Moreover, holistic education seeks to be inclusive of different educational approaches (transmission, transaction, and transformation) that are presently operative in schools. Finally, Miller argues that holistic education is about a deliberate movement away from fragmentation to seeking connections between various fields and spheres (Miller, 1993, pp.3-15).

In my view contemplation is consistent with the aims of holistic education. The contemplative attentiveness to the underlying unity that exists in the universe is consistent with holism's goal of seeking connections across different fields. Contemplation does not negate the reality of differentiation and specification. Quite the contrary. However, a contemplative understanding of the world recognizes that the principle of differentiation is a function of the primal energy that is rooted in the fundamental unity in the universe. The goal of contemplation is to see, to wonder at, and to behold the presence of the underlying unity that permeates all being. Seeing this unity permits one to see the connection between polarities and to see the unity beyond dualism that exists in reality too. Having apprehended the underlying unity the contemplative is then able to consciously balance the various pieces of our fragmented world. Moreover, the contemplative is able to bring a heart that is open and inclusive to all areas of life. A contemplative can, and at times must, discriminate so as to clarify and judge, but the fundamental stance of a contemplative is to seek connections, be inclusive, and to promote balance and harmony.

Ron Miller has argued that while we need to attend to spirituality, we cannot try to "train children for monastic practice" (Miller, 1997, p.29). He argues that in holism spirituality cannot be seen as something otherworldly but rather must be seen as pertaining to helping people make sense of the many layers of wholeness and meaning that comprise the human being. Indeed, he contends that we cannot talk about spirituality today without also talking about democracy, social justice, racial and class oppression, and the need for a sustainable environmental orientation (Miller, 1997, p.28). Miller is correct in that spirituality today must embrace the concerns of everyday life if it is to be at all credible. Moreover, spirituality must include the areas of poverty, justice, equality, economics, and politics. In particular, contemplation must include these areas of human life. Otherwise the contemplative claim to an underlying unity will have limited or dubious validity for if such a unity can only be found in an inner, contemplative awareness and never in the outer world of culture and institutions, then questions need to be raised as to the truth and relevance of contemplation. Ultimately, the contemplative awareness of the unity of being in life, if it is understood as including social and political areas, can contribute to a holistic way of being in the world. Thus, when the social and political areas are included within contemplation the possibility for a healthier and more holistic spirituality emerges.

Contemplation and Action

Few, except perhaps for cloistered monks and nuns, live lives totally devoted to contemplation. The professional contemplative vocation is not my concern here. I am concerned with the contemplative dimension as it is available in everyday life and I contend that there is a contemplative dimension to human life. However, the fact that we are human beings means that we are social beings who find ourselves in communities and for whom action is a constitutive component of living. Thus, we work, play, travel, love, and laugh and through each of these avenues we express our selves. This active dimension is essential to a balanced life. Indeed, as Beck has argued, the active areas of life must be part of any spirituality (Beck, 1990, p.165).

A contemplative-in-action spirituality strives to integrate the active and contemplative dimensions of life. Through such integration the fruits of one's active life are brought to one's contemplation and the fruits of one's contemplation are brought to one's active life. Eventually, we come to understand that, from a viewpoint of a contemplative-in-action, there are few sharp distinctions between action and contemplation. Buchmann, in reflecting upon the role of contemplation with the busy life of teaching, referred to Thomas Aquinas's position on the integration of action and contemplation.

> Thomas Aquinas therefore concludes that teaching sometimes belongs to the active life and sometimes to the contemplative life. Yet, in moving from contemplation to action in teaching, we do not subtract the contemplative but add the active dimension. Put differently, teaching is not a life of action tempered by occasional fits of abstractions, but, in the words of St. Thomas, the active life in teaching 'proceeds from the fullness of contemplation'. (Buchmann, 1989, p.54)

Yet, despite the integration advocated by contemplation-in-action, our culture values action more than contemplation. We do this because our Western culture values possessions, work, and social standing as indicators of personal worth much more than a person's capacity for wonder, awe, and relationship, capacities assisted through contemplation.

> You are expected to produce, to make something which is not you, something which can be objectified, and through money made

> available and interchangeable. You have to earn what you consume,
> in addition to your reputation and privileges, or you will be looked
> down upon as a worthless parasite.... Nothing is gratuitous, comes as
> a gift, 'gratuities' are taxable income! (Panikkar, 1981, p.265)

Perhaps Panikkar overstates the problem here. But, he does point to the cultural and economic pressures that can drive a person away from a contemplative attention to being. Such pressures are readily apparent in the world of work where most often the context is not conducive to a contemplative stance (Buchmann, 1989, p.48), although there is a great need for contemplative practice to be integrated within the work world today (Whyte, 1994, pp.98-99). Much of the problem of our present education system can be located in its preoccupation with the active dimension of preparation for work without integrating the awareness of the need for relationships, connections, and communion.

Now, despite the critique of the glorification of action in our Western world, I do not want to place contemplation above action. What is needed is the integration of being and action.

> Though the active life and the contemplative life can be
> distinguished, both are forms of human life, and in an actual existence
> now one, now the other, form will predominate. And it is possible for
> action to lead to contemplation and for contemplation to lead to
> action: both forms of life are complementary. (Buchmann, 1989,
> p.49)

Since many of our contemporary problems can be traced to a faulty, fractured, and incomplete knowing perpetuated by disconnected rationalism the contemplative search for underlying unity can act as a corrective to such an imbalance. Moreover, contemplation, because it leads to and is fed by action, can help balance our fixation on action. Contemplation-in-action seeks to avoid any unhealthy activism, or quietism for that matter, by upholding both dimensions as equality important for a balanced and holistic life.

In our day there is a need to broaden our understanding of the active dimension to include the social, economic, cultural, and political realms. As indicated above, if contemplation is about holism it must include the areas of justice, equality, peace, and ecology. These are not only areas of life that impact on the practical lives of individuals but also on the consciousness of individuals. A new consciousness is being born due to rapid advances in communication technology and the saturation of our individual and collective psyches by the mass media. Indeed, a new global consciousness is emerging. Spirituality today must take into account this new development. This new consciousness must be integrated into the active and contemplative dimensions of any spirituality today that wants to be credible. Hence, to push the understanding of the active dimension beyond the realm of work, leisure, relationships, etc. I think it is important to incorporate liberating praxis as a necessary dimension for contemplation-in-action. This will be the subject of the next chapter.

Suffice it to say that what we need today are contemplatives with a global consciousness. Such contemplatives would not divide people into secular or religious but would seek to meet all people with a deep respect due to each person's capacity to behold the underlying unity to the universe. Such contemplatives would be both male and female who could dialogue across the differences between genders because of an appreciation for the connection to the other. Such contemplatives would reject any manipulation of the natural world that would harm nature precisely because it would harm the ground of all being that connects the natural and human worlds. Such contemplatives, if living within religious traditions, would feel comfortable when invited to the home of those of other faiths. Finally, such contemplatives would use science and technology to foster balance, inclusion, and connection with all of reality.

Conclusion

I have argued for an appreciation of the mystical or contemplative dimension of life with a view to recovering the richness found in this dimension which is so often ignored in our Western culture. The contemplative dimension is found within all world religions but is also innate to the human person. As such it can provide a foundational spirituality, one in which non-religious and religious can share. I would even go so far as to say that it has universal applications in that it can be embraced by peoples of all genders, races, and religions. It is a spirituality that can assist in the reversal of the course of ecological devastation to which traditional spiritualities have contributed. It can be a truly inclusive and ecologically responsive spirituality.

The contemplative dimension of the human person is concerned with an attitude or a consciousness that is open, receptive, and attentive to beholding reality in all its fullness and beauty. Such an approach can counteract the imbalance found in techno-rationality that permeates our culture. It is an approach that appreciates the importance of relationships, intuitions, emotions, and the inter-relatedness between all beings. Also, it is consistent with a holistic approach to life, for in its attentiveness to unity in being it can assist in the promotion of balance, inclusion, and connectivity in all areas of life.

But the contemplative dimension does not stand alone. It must be lived in conjunction with the active dimension. This active dimension today includes not only the realm of personal action as found in work, art, leisure, family life, and so on. It must also include the realm of the social and the communal for today, unlike ever before, we are aware of the impact which culture, economics, politics, and religion have upon our daily lives. As such, a contemplative-in-action spirituality must include the area of liberating praxis in order to be truly holistic, effective, and credible. It is to this concern that we now turn our attention.

CHAPTER THREE

THE ACTIVE DIMENSION OF LIBERATING PRAXIS

So a new kind of spiritual exercise is emerging. It involves not
withdrawal but engagement; not shutting one's eyes to evil but
opening one's eyes to see both the individual and systemic reasons for
that evil; not emptying the mind, so that the Spirit can flood into the
emptiness, but filling the mind with statistics about who doesn't eat
and why not, about where concentrations of wealth (and consequent
injustice) are located, about indignities suffered by powerless people,
so that the Spirit can be well informed in using the new saints in
subsequent assaults on centers of exploitation and unjust privilege.
(Robert McAfee Brown, 1988, p.116)

Throughout history there has been a concern with the problem of dualism in

spirituality. There has always been a tendency to divorce private and public, inner

and outer, individual and communal realms. Western culture continues to work out

of this dualism and it is precisely this problem which has contributed to the difficulty

of articulating a holistic and healthy spirituality for our times. Contemplation-in-

action provides a method for moving beyond dualism, but this method needs to be

reconstituted in light of our global world. In this chapter I attend to the active

dimension, particularly the area of social and political action. Any spirituality that

purports to be holistic must include political action for social transformation as both

an expression and a source of one's spiritual life. Thus, a person who pursues social

justice is more effective and satisfied if they support their political action with

contemplation. Also, the person who contemplates is more effective and satisfied if

they support their contemplation with political action.

69

I will begin this chapter with a discussion of politics and the problem of justice with a view to disclosing some of the philosophical problems encountered when questions of justice arise. I will discuss our need for an appropriate cosmology that is responsive to the problems of our times, particularly with regard to justice. This will be followed by a presentation supportive of a liberating praxis approach that brings the active dimension into a dialogue with reflection. Finally, I shall point to the place of contemplation in the method of liberating praxis. My aim in this chapter is to situate liberating praxis as a constitutive and necessary dimension of a holistic spirituality for our time.

Politics and the Problem of Justice

Attention to culture, to community, and embeddedness in one's 'context' is a positive feature of our postmodern politics. Indeed, the work of post-modernists to break free of the Euro-centric hegemonies of transcendental and universal precepts has proven fruitful and the political and cultural diversity that flourishes throughout the globe is invigorating and sustaining. However, an ironic consequence of this turn to the local is a diminishment of any claims to a common universal worldview precisely when what is needed today is a comprehensive and global framework from which to approach contemporary social and political problems. From a political orientation, then, the curtailing of universal principles has not resulted in the end of social and political injustices. On the other hand, the upholding of universal principals such of justice, equality, and liberty have not been universally applied often because of authoritarian imposition or disrespect for local cultures. North American society struggles with knowing how to include social justice within politics, how to articulate a common understanding of what constitutes justice, and how to organize society around principles of justice. More often than not questions of justice are considered inconsistent with politics in any practical and transformative sense. These difficulties are rooted in Western political culture that seems incapable of adequately interfacing the value of personal autonomy with the value of social justice. Questions of social justice, then, invariably involve questions of politics.

Benhabib has traced our contemporary problematic to the debate between the Enlightenment libertarian tradition and the neo-Aristotelian or neo-Hegelian communitarianism. She argues that the only way to avoid the evils of liberalism (loss of values, alienation, civility, etc.) and communalism (fundamentalism, totalitarianism, loss of individualism, etc.) is to work towards a procedural ethics that upholds the principles of universal moral respect and egalitarian reciprocity (Benhabib, 1990, pp.2-8). While I agree with Benhabib's analysis of our present impasse I am not convinced that her articulation of a procedural ethics based on universal precepts is adequate for the task of social justice. It seems to me that she fails to fully comprehend the magnitude of disputes that rage in our world, the crucial issue of power politics, and the disparities that actually do exists between peoples, cultures, and worldviews.

Elsewhere, Eamonn Callan has argued that our present problems with universal norms can be traced to an inappropriate understanding of the concept of justice given the reality of pluralism. Callan rejects the libertarian notion of justice, exemplified by Rawls, as undermining the values and energy of pluralist society because of its tendency to absolutize or to impose a uniformity of fairness in contexts where such uniformity cannot exist. At the same time, Callan rejects the communitarian notion of justice as unworkable as well because of the "limits it imposes upon diversity" (Callan, 1991, p.72). For Callan the corrective to both the libertarian and communitarian approaches is a recovery of patriotism augmented by compassion and imagination.

> Patriotism is identification with others in the ongoing life of a political community. The patriot is someone who looks ahead into a future where she hopes her community will persist and prosper, and also behind into the past of her people, a past which, by virtue of identification with her fellow citizens, becomes integral to her own story as well. (Callan, 1991, p.75)

I am not convinced that patriotism provides an adequate resolution to the problem of liberalism or communalism. Within democracy, people espousing radically different political ideologies, some which are outright dismissive of the appeal to community that Callan wants, can still claim to be patriots. Moreover, within a globalized economy appeals to patriotism appear to be of limited efficacy when applied to questions of justice because one feature of globalization is a movement beyond the nation state as the single or primary affiliation for people.

It seems to me that both Callan and Benhabib are grappling with one of the crucial contemporary political questions: how to pursue justice while simultaneously encouraging a healthy pluralism within a global context. Benhabib's communicative ethics and Callan's appeal to patriotism are partial solutions. However, more is required.

Alan Brown, in *Modern Political Philosophy* (1986), has picked up this disquiet within the contemporary discourse on politics and focused on the question of justice. He argues that modern political philosophy suffers from two basic failures: i) an inability to articulate an adequate theory of the human good around which societies ought to be organized, and ii) an inability to articulate an adequate theory of justice to govern the distribution of the good (Brown, 1986, pp.131-132). Appealing to Aristotle's naturalism, Brown argues that 'the good' includes "physical and mental health, material affluence (within limits), the development of some of one's potential, useful or "meaningful" work, a set of personal relationships (friendship, love, etc.) and, to regulate these, a rational plan of life to be lived in a rational organised society" (Brown, 1986, p.136). For Brown, the good society is a society which permits and promotes the individual attainment of these realities.

Brown's pragmatism is evident when he argues that such a society does not truly exist because we have too many people who do not have even the basics for his conception of the good life. From North American society, Galbraith has pointed out that it is the 'contented majority' who, exercising their democratic rights, continue to support an economic system that is built upon the poverty of what he calls the 'functional underclass'. This functional underclass is comprised of the poor, the unemployed, the underemployed, welfare recipients, and seasonal laborers. This class "serves the living standard and the comfort of the more favored community" (Galbraith, 1992, p.31). Galbraith argues that the North American myth of upward mobility can hold no promise for the underclass because the opportunities for advancement have been severely curtailed due to middle class resistance to higher taxation in support of social programs and the preferred expenditure towards the military (Galbraith, 1992, pp.122-143). Both Brown and Galbraith agree that a truly just society does not exist.

Alan Brown argues that what is needed to correct injustice towards the good is a social system where everyone is provided with the basic goods even if this puts limits on others' ability to pursue and acquire non-essential goods. His principle is as follows:

> If a social structure systematically denies to some the possibility of enjoying some or all of the basic goods then it is to be improved upon, if possible. An improvement would be a system which provides more people with the basic goods at the cost of denying others inessential goods. (Brown, 1986, p.167)

Standing on such a premise Brown argues that societies in which inequalities exist are unreasonable since the social relations are destructive to the good life of all concerned, poor and rich alike. Brown dismisses laissez-faire capitalism as ultimately destructive of the common good and argues in favor of "market socialism" as the best vehicle for the promotion of a good and just society (Brown, 1986, p.168).

From within the emerging field of political theology there is a consistent attempt to integrate the pursuit of justice within politics with the added investigative tool of theology. While it can be argued that this field is "still barely nascent and has scarcely reached the level of methodological refinement" (Haight, 1985, p.15), it cannot be denied that the attempt to intelligently interface the concerns of politics, justice, and religion is a necessary endeavor for our times. Political theology is based on the recognition that "every theology has a political context" and that each culture will express its theology differently (Nolan, 1991, p.5-7). Moreover, while different theologies can be in dialogue one cannot automatically transpose the theology from one context to another. This is particularly true when North Americans try to borrow from "Third World" liberation theologies because, as Fox says, the "contexts of the "First" and "Third" worlds differ so vastly (Fox, 1991, p. xi).

Leddy has suggested that Canadians have yet to truly begin to claim their own location and voice and to create their own political theology. I would agree with this observation. We tend to borrow from the United States and more particularly from Latin America. While some Canadian theologians have articulated a socially responsive theology of praxis from a Canadian perspective, the truth is that we are just beginning to create a truly Canadian political theology (Leddy, 1987, pp.128-129).

Baum has also been cognizant of this difficulty and has argued that Canadians cannot too quickly transpose the theoretical tools from another culture to Canada.

Baum argues that the North American political context is unique in that, unlike Latin America where much of the suffering of the poor and marginalized can be attributed to classism and oppression, the social structures which create human suffering in North America are more complex. He contends that this requires a more detailed analysis of the social reality.

> It is unrealistic, in my view, to look for a single form of oppression in North America, to which all others are subordinated. What we have is a complex intermeshing of technocratic depersonalization and immobility, economic domination and exploitation, racial exclusion and inferiorization, and other forms including the subjugation of women. ... the analysis of social sin in North America will inevitably be complex. (Baum, 1975, pp.218-219)

Now, on the one hand Baum's reticence to wholeheartedly accept a simple scenario of domination and oppression, which Paulo Friere has stated is the root cause of injustice (Freire, 1970, pp.127-133), is understandable. North American society is complex and the causes of injustices are often multiple rather than singular. At the same time North American political theology has something unique to offer due to both the complexity of the culture and the global influence which that culture holds.

> In conclusion, the noetic praxis of political theology in North America will involve an extensive collaboration within contexts characterized by a global perspective. A global perspective is intrinsic to political theology in the United States insofar as economic and political life in the United States is itself intrinsically global in its effects and consequences. (Lamb, 1982, p.21)

Hence, precisely because of the influence of American culture, which has and continues to influence Canadian culture and politics, it is imperative that the lens of political theology be brought to bear on questions of justice. As North Americans uncover the causes of social injustices in their own location and dialogue with similar people engaged in the same task throughout the world, perhaps a more just and equitable global ethic will emerge.

The Need for a Cosmological Framework

Baum's caution regarding simplistic analysis is wise. We do need to appreciate the complexity and intermingling of various causes and implications of injustice in North America. In order to understand our situation we need first to articulate some larger perspective in which the questions of justice, politics, and action can be asked.

What is missing today is an appropriate 'cosmology' for our time. We need a cosmology that seeks to see how various locations of injustice are created and related. Moreover, as Berry and Fox have advocated, we need a cosmology that places the questions of justice within the human community in the larger context of the earth and upholds community and interrelatedness as a hermeneutic backdrop for our time.

The cosmology that is presently operative in our Western world is incomplete. That is, our Western world's fixation on techno-rationalism as the overarching philosophical approach to life is a partial cosmology. Science and technology, standing on their own, have led to a partial way of knowing and ultimately a partial understanding of society. When science and technology are presented as the prevailing and only valid philosophies for our world, then our ability to resolve contemporary problems is reduced not only because the Western worldview has been brought into contest with other worldviews but also because within the Western world the techno-rational approach fails to provide all the tools for a comprehensive and holistic solution to Western problems. What is needed is a wider, more comprehensive view of learning and of life itself.

I agree with authors such as Oliver, Whitehead, Fox, and Berry that we need to discover a cosmology that can cross various fields of knowledge.

> We have now arrived at the central theme of this book. It is the search for a conception of education which would move us to generate imaginative scenarios of positive culture, whole visions which might direct us both to feel and critically examine the depth and breadth of human experience – qualities of becoming; qualities of being; qualities of knowing; qualities of participation and connection. We see the essential flaw in modernity as its inability to generate such visions in the midst of the fragments of its incredibly successful machines. ...
>
> What might we call such a venture that would embrace the various fields of knowing – metaphysics, science, religious intuition, the arts, history? We would propose the word cosmology... (Oliver, 1989, p.55)

A cosmological or worldview approach calls for a view that seeks the connections and interrelatedness between various areas of our world. It also seeks to integrate reflection with personal commitment and prudent action. A cosmologist, in keeping with modernists and postmodernists, sees oneself as a participant in the ongoing creation of the universe (Oliver, 1989, pp.56-58).

Oliver argues in favour of Whitehead's concept of cosmology and sees no contradiction between cosmology and grounded culture. Indeed, he argues that there exists a homeostatic balance between separateness of cultures and the unity of being found in cosmology (Oliver, 1989, p.58). Moreover, the paradox or incoherence between cosmology and culture can only be lifted if we acknowledge that the term cosmology is ambiguous in itself and refers to both general and concrete levels of grounded cultural experiences (Oliver, 1989, pp.59-60). In a sense, the more one is grounded in one's context the more connected one will feel to the universe. Oliver argues that he is not advocating some grand new religion but rather a balance between individuality, community, and universality (Oliver, 1989, p.63). The phrase 'think globally, act locally' comes to mind here as representative of a cosmological awareness.

Matthew Fox echoes a similar approach when he argues that cosmology is about our attempt to understand the cosmos through science, mysticism, and art (Fox, 1991, p.56). He also argues that an appeal to cosmology does not negate the need to attend to one's local context. On the contrary, it is in the local context of culture that one seeks liberation (Fox, 1991, p.70).

Thomas Berry has argued that what we need today is a 'functional cosmology', one that takes the earth as the origin of all life and takes this origin seriously. Human beings can no longer continue to understand their existence outside the context of the earth itself. More importantly the survival of the human species is intricately connected to the survival of the planet.

> Neither humans as a species nor any of our activities can be understood in any significant manner except in our role in the functioning of the earth and of the universe itself. We come into existence, have our present meaning, and attain our destiny within this numinous context, for the universe in its every phase is numinous in its depths. (Berry, 1990, p.87)

Berry argues that the present religious traditions are not up to the task of articulating and pursuing a cosmology that is ecologically responsive. In particular, the Christian religion is too locked into a concern with afterlife and transcendence to be adequately engaged in the here and now. Other eco-theologians have echoed

Berry's mistrust of institutional religions. Freda Rajotte, for example, has pointed out that "much of traditional church teaching was rooted in a dualistic approach and in arrogant anthroprocentrism, in which humans alone were thought to possess souls" (Rajotte, 1990, p.10). Berry argues that we need to allow the new story of the universe to instruct us as to how to integrate the human and earth activities within a consciousness of numinous presence in the world.

Berry calls for a cosmology of relatedness wherein everything in the universe is connected. This interrelatedness means that nothing can be complete on its own. Absolute autonomy and separateness is an illusion that is unmasked when one attends to the underpinnings of reality. Berry's insight is particularly challenging to North Americans who highly prize autonomy often to the detriment of society at large.

Contemporary physicists support the view that the universe is made of "an interconnected web of relations" that is intrinsically dynamic (Capra, 1982, p.87). It appears that even from within the purely scientific field there is an emerging awareness of the relatedness and connection that exists in all of life.

> Every contemporary physicist, however, will accept the main theme of the presentation – that modern physics has transcended the mechanistic Cartesian view of the world and is leading us to a holistic and intrinsically dynamic conception of the universe. (Capra, 1982, pp.96-97)

As Berry says, the universe is a communion and community of interconnected parts, each of which is seeking to become conscious of the whole in which all life participates (Berry, 1990, p.91).

> The interrelatedness of the universe in its every manifestation is what establishes the unity of the entire world and enables it to be a "universe". Every atomic particle is immediately present to every other atomic particle in a manner that enables us to say that the volume of each atom is the volume of the universe. This mutual presence is the full complexity of its living and nonliving forms. Without such intercommunion nothing would ever happen. (Berry, 1990, p.121)

Now, despite the dangers of misplaced concreteness and over-generalization inherent in any attempt to develop a category of the whole or the universe, there is merit in trying to enunciate a cosmological perspective. We do think with 'worldviews' or 'philosophies of life' and these inevitably come into play in the many areas of human interaction. Freire himself has argued that our consciousness is constituted by generative themes and that each culture presents a 'thematic universe' into which it enculturates its citizens (Freire, 1970, pp.92-95). A 'thematic universe' is akin to the term cosmology for it purports to explain the largest picture for the learner.

In our emerging global consciousness there is a need to discuss the question of cosmologies and be cognizant of the cosmologies that arise from different cultural and religious locations. But, more urgently than simply becoming cognizant and tolerant of difference, which is the postmodern legacy, I agree with Berry that there is an urgency that requires us to move beyond quiet tolerance and dismissive relativism to an awareness that is rooted in what concerns us all. We must begin to reconstruct a cosmology with a view that "universality must be built up from below and not imposed from above" (Nolan, 1991, p.16). In this regard, I think that Berry's call for an understanding of cosmology as the universe story is timely and wise.

Dunn has argued that Berry has challenged us to move beyond our anthroprocentricism towards a new cosmology wherein we recognize "the larger earth community, not the human community, as normative as regards reality and value" (Dunn, 1990, p.36). What this requires is a recognition that the earth community, the relatedness of all species, including human, must become "the essential springboard for knowing what we are about" (Dunn, 1990, p.42). Any 'thematic universe', 'worldview', or 'cosmology' must be stretched to include such an expansive recognition.

In my view we need such a cosmological perspective to provide a backdrop or framework for political and liberating action. Too often attempts are made to address single issues without any appeal to the foundational or connected issues that are also involved. For example, questions of economic justice need to be connected to the accompanying concerns of sexism, classism, racism, war, exploitation, religious fanaticism, etc. Ultimately each area of injustice is also connected with the way the human community is treating the earth. The beauty of an ecologically centered cosmology is that it is the one area of life in which all people have a vested interest. Simply put, if the earth dies, we all die.

I see the value of a cosmology of the larger earth community to be valuable because it calls for a consciousness of relatedness, connectedness, and community. I think that it is precisely the inability to be conscious of the relatedness of social concerns, the connectedness between one social injustice and another, and the community of communities that constitutes our global world that is one of the reasons why transformative social actions are so often dismissed or depleted of efficacy. What we require is a new consciousness, a global consciousness, to support the political consciousness of people. We require a consciousness that would permit a more honest approach to redistributive economics and the crossing of the borders between rich and poor. A cosmological consciousness would provide a framework for such an orientation, for it would be large enough to be responsive to the complexity of the social justice issues of today as well as require practical engagement in action at the local level.

Praxis and Liberation

Having discussed politics and justice and the need for a cosmology to form the backdrop to political action, we now need to turn to the question of political action itself. Picking up on DeRoo's "the road to holiness passes through the road of action" (DeRoo, 1991, p.36), the domain of social and political action can be brought within the sphere of spirituality. If action is a necessary and legitimate part of a healthy spirituality then political action and social justice are necessary and legitimate spheres of engagement. Political engagement requires an orientation of liberating praxis, a method that includes action and critical reflection oriented towards liberation from injustice. This method stands upon two important presumptions, the recovery of human subjectivity within history and the option for solidarity. I shall discuss these two important foundational presumptions before discussing the praxis method of reflection and action.

Freire, in his *Pedagogy of the Oppressed* (1970), takes up a twentieth century turn to the human person as the subject of history rather than the object of history. The world in which a person lives is not a closed system into which one adapts but rather an open system ongoingly created by human beings.

> Friere is able to do this because he operates on one basic assumption:
> that man's ontological vocation (as he calls it) is to be a Subject who
> acts upon and transforms his world, and in so doing moves towards
> ever new possibilities for fuller and richer life individually and

collectively. This world to which he relates is not a static and closed
order, a given reality which man must accept and to which he must
adjust; rather, it is a problem to be worked on and solved. (Friere,
1970, pp.12-13)

Freire claims that every human person has a vocation to create history by humanizing
the world (Freire, 1970, p.28). This vocation to transform the world is one in which
the individual person is transformed as well for there is a dialectic between the
personal and the social (Gadotti, 1996, p.xvii).

The recovery of the potency of human subjectivity results in a recovery of
personal power because once a person begins to act responsibly to change and
humanize their particular socio-economic context they can retrieve power which
previously had been, consciously or unconsciously, given over to organizational
systems. The use of power "ought to be used with and for people in the interest of
hope and freedom" (Butkus, 1989, p.572). That is, power related to social structures
must be activated with the view to social and communal benefits. Otherwise, power
is used only for private purposes, which in the final analysis does not liberate
communities. The move towards historical subjectivity and the location of political
power within the communal sphere is a philosophical precondition for liberating
praxis for without a departure from the view of the world as fixed and immutable and
without an appreciation of the capacity of persons, in community, to bring about
change within their social contexts, the probability of moving towards actions that
transform and liberate is limited.

Liberating praxis presumes human solidarity. Departing from the
Enlightenment legacy of the autonomous individual, the task of solidarity demands
an appreciation of the connection and mutuality between individuals and
communities. The human being becomes a person through relationships and in

community. This view has not formed the overarching ethos of Canadian and American societies for North American culture is an outgrowth of the Enlightenment project. Bellah and his colleagues situate the numerous North American social problems in the trap of individualism.

> What has failed at every level – from the society of nations to the national society to the local community to the family – is integration: we have failed to remember "our community as members of the same body," as John Winthrop put it. We have committed what to the republican founders of our nation was a cardinal sin: we have put our own good, as individuals, as groups, as a nation, ahead of the common good. (Bellah, Madsen, Sullivan, Swidler, and Tipton, 1986, p.285)

In reaction to this flaw within North American culture there is a coalescing of voices advocating a return to relatedness, community, and solidarity. Some feminists have argued that justice must be balanced with care lived within community (Gilligan, 1982, pp.59-63; Noddings, 1986, pp.79-103). Callan has stated that the complementarity between justice and care stands upon the recognition that the advancement of one's good is directly connected to that of others. "In caring for someone unselfishly... that advancement of her good becomes partly constitutive of one's own good, so that when hers is thwarted, other things being equal, so too is one's own." (Callan, 1992, p.440) Elsewhere, White points out that feminists in their call for attention to intersubjectivity argue that this demands that "one draw the other into one's own interpretive frame" (White, 1991, p.99). Some feminists, then, actively call for solidarity between people as an antidote to the alienation found in Western culture.

This call for solidarity is also found within political theology in its hermeneutical concept of the 'preferential option for the poor'. Baum points out that this option has two dimensions:

> The option is first of all a perspective for seeing the world. The option commits us to read society from the perspective of its victims. ...What the option for the poor asks of middle-class people is to abandon their own class perspective and read society from below, through the eyes of the people at the bottom and in the margin. But the option for the poor has a second, an activist, dimension. It includes solidarity with the poor and their struggle for justice. It calls for action and public witness. What is presupposed here is that the poor ... are to be the agents of their own liberation. All who love justice, therefore, from whatever class, must support the poor in their struggle for liberation. (Baum, 1987, pp.28-29)

The preferential option for the poor is a hermeneutical tool for solidarity and action with and for the marginalized within a society. It stands on a 'reading' of or a listening to the effects of social structures as they are experienced by the dispossessed and marginalized. Fox goes so far as to argue that this hermeneutical option for the poor can be applied to ecology because in tracing our origins to the earth we can recognize our 'poverty' and dependence upon others (Fox, 1991, p.29). The preferential option for the poor is compatible with the call of feminists to attend to the needs of the other and the requirement for solidarity as a precondition for authentic transformative action.

There is a dialectic between contemplation and action that needs to be reformulated within a structural approach. Here my concern is with the active dimension as lived within social and political action. Based on a cosmology of relatedness and connection and keeping my eyes on the need for justice, I want to argue for liberating praxis as a legitimate field of endeavor for individuals who seek to express their spirituality in ways that are socially and politically responsive.

The word 'praxis' comes from the Greek meaning 'action'. I am using the term here in its radical sense of 'transformative action' (Gadotti, 1996, p.xvii), in which one seeks to transform social structures rather than the 'reformist' approach which seeks to put cultures back on track with their foundations (Hall and Sullivan, p.11). Praxis includes consciousness, practice, and reflection on practice (Willets, 1995, p.11), and is a method that seeks to honor action as a legitimate and necessary locus for learning. "Praxis is, then, the natural state of human beings who attempt to be self-reflective about their own actions" (Gadotti, 1996, p. xxiii). Now, while all learning can be 'potentially subversive activity' (Jarvis, 1987, p.18), this is particularly true of transformative praxis. For the intention of such praxis is not the renewal of society as it is but the advocacy of the abandonment of the 'formatively inappropriate' structures of society in favor of alternative structures that include the marginalized and dispossessed segments of society (Hall and Sullivan, p.11).

My choice is to use the term 'liberating praxis' as opposed to 'transformative praxis'. While I embrace the approach of transformation I think that liberation is an acceptable word for the area of justice with which I am concerned. We do need to transform society and the structures that impede the full participation of the dispossessed. Liberation, however, speaks of a movement out of captivity to freedom.

> ... liberation is pursued chiefly to establish a new social order that will wipe out the oppressive structures to which disadvantaged people have been subjected and create a society where all, and not just some, can live creative lives. (Brown, 1988, p.16)

For the purposes of my study, liberation is a movement of leaving behind the captivity of division, separateness, and individualism and moving towards liberation found in connection, relatedness, and community. Only when we begin to see the problems of social injustice as rooted in a consciousness of separation and individualism and begin to work within a cosmological consciousness of connection, relationship, and community can we begin to hope for the amelioration of disparities in our culture. Freedom lies, then, not in individualism, but in an understanding that authentic personhood is lived in community and through actions that promote the common good. Liberation involves movement towards a cosmology of the earth community in which questions of the common good are asked and a society where the basic needs of all, as articulated by Alan Brown in his concept of the just society, are met. Liberating praxis is concerned with reflective action towards this end. This is a legitimate task for education today for "education as the practice of freedom is not just about liberating knowledge, it's about liberating practice" (hooks, 1994, p.147).

Freire claims that his praxis method is for radicals who are committed to the liberation of the oppressed (Freire, 1970, p.24). Liberation is achieved through a process of 'conscientization' in which a person becomes aware of the social, political, and economic structures that impact upon their concrete situation. The process of conscientization involves the investigation of the generative themes operative within people's concrete reality. 'Generative themes', which contribute to the 'thematic universe' (or cosmology) of participants, contain the ideas, values, hopes, and challenges which a people hold in their culture. Freire states that generative themes move from the general to the particular, from the universal to the local. The fundamental theme of our time, according to Freire, is that of domination and the opposite theme of liberation.

Individuals investigate the generative themes with a view to discovering the oppressive structures embedded in their culture. Their discovery assists in a gradual emergence from oppression and leads to practical interventions in their historical reality to remove the oppression. The process of conscientization leads to liberation for the oppressed who acquire the skills to learn and act independently (Freire, 1970, pp.92-118). According to Freire, then, a transformed consciousness will lead to actions which liberate.

In some North American contexts the term 'social analysis' is more commonly used than 'conscientization'.

> Social analysis can be defined as the effort to obtain a more complete picture of a social situation by exploring its historical and structural relationships. (Holland and Henriot, 1980, p.5)

The goal of social analysis is the same as Freire's conscientization: to bring about a change in the consciousness of the participants. The transformation of consciousness demands a critique and dismantling of the dominant consciousness with a view to nurturing an alternative consciousness which serves people and communities living in solidarity (Brueggemann, 1978, p.13).

Freire's method is cyclical in that it calls for participants to continually reflect upon their actions and to explore the root causes of injustices so as to ongoingly transform society. This dialectic between action and reflection is central to the praxis pedagogy and has the effect of democratizing education.

Liberating Praxis and Contemplation

The strength of the liberating praxis method lies in the symbiotic connection between action and reflection. True learning takes place when action and reflection are kept in constant tension and dialogue. As Freire has pointed out verbalism and activism rarely bring about a transformation in real conditions (Freire, 1970, pp.52-53). The truly effective activist is one who has reflected deeply on structural issues. Conversely, the truly effective thinker is one who is engaged in practical action rooted in solidarity with others. The dialectic between reflection and action, theory and practice, is one of the reasons transforming praxis is so effective as an educational method.

The method of liberating praxis complements the traditional way of contemplative-in-action. Freire himself saw the importance of openness and deep listening to avoid sectarian indoctrination (Freire, 1970, p.23). The open and listening stance of Freire's radical approach is akin to the contemplative stance of beholding and attending. In fact, the reflective moment when radicals seek to 'deconstruct' their social context, whether through 'social analysis' or 'conscientization', is an appropriate moment for contemplation.

Since contemplation involves attentiveness and openness to reality, there is no reason to think the contemplative dimension could not be a welcome addition to critical reflection. Critical reflection, social analysis, conscientization all run the danger of being works of the intellect. Contemplation, although inclusive of the intellect, seeks to involve the whole person in their knowing. As such, contemplation can assist in bringing a depth and expanse to the reflection moment of praxis. Contemplation can bring a necessary piece to the praxis method that has been missing.

Moreover, a contemplative seeks to discover the connections, relatedness, and unity that exist in reality. The activist working with a cosmological consciousness also seeks to create a society based on connections, relatedness, and community. Thus, contemplatives and activists share the same horizon of connection, relatedness, and community. When both dimensions are found within one person then a truly integrated approach to life is possible.

The dialectic found between action and reflection in praxis methodology is similar to the integration of action and contemplation advocated by St. Ignatius of Loyola. Because of this contemplation-in-liberating praxis is a method that could also be called a political or justice spirituality.

Conclusion

Those who engage in social justice work within North America are often aware that the causes of injustice are usually multiple. While there may be ample evidence of domination and oppression or privilege and marginalization, very often social injustices are complicated by various contributing factors such as sexism, classism, racism, ageism, and militarism. Deconstructing the root causes of injustice is further complicated in North America by an embeddedness in a notion of personal freedom as autonomy at the expense of social responsibility. Coupled with this is the erosion of an acceptable definition of the 'common good' within the sphere of politics. The result is a situation in which is it difficult to act for justice.

In order to move beyond these difficulties we are in need of developing a cosmology of relatedness, connection, and community. The cosmology of the earth as a community as suggested by contemporary ecologists provides a credible framework for addressing questions of justice. When we begin to be conscious of the connection, relatedness, and community that can exist between the 'haves' and the 'have-nots', and that the well-being of the 'other' is intricately connected to not only my own well-being but the well-being of the earth itself, then it becomes possible to engage in actions to promote justice. Working from a cosmological consciousness can assist in overcoming the fractured approaches presently operative within our culture.

John MacMurray once wrote, "all knowledge is for the sake of action, and all meaningful action for the sake of friendship" (MacMurray, 1953, p.15). The method of liberating praxis moves in the direction of placing knowledge at the service of political action for justice and community. If we begin to move beyond seeing meaningful action as only for the personal realm and include the social and political realms, we can see that all meaningful action is for the sake of social justice. As Freire claims, education is for the practice of freedom.

Liberating praxis is a necessary component of contemplation-in-action. It adds to the traditional Ignatian ideal of the integration of contemplation and action our contemporary awareness of social structure, place, and history. As such, liberating praxis is a welcome addition to this spiritual method. At the same time, contemplation serves to sustain and complement the lives of those engaged in a liberating praxis method. It permits spirituality to be intelligently and persuasively brought into the sphere of politics and justice by adding a deeper dimension that is often overlooked.

I have argued for liberating praxis as a constitutive dimension of spirituality in this chapter in order to develop the active side of the contemplative-in-action approach. But how the active and contemplative dimensions actually relate within a social and political context needs to be developed further. This is the task of dialectics and is the concern of the next chapter.

CHAPTER FOUR

CONTEMPLATION-IN-LIBERATING PRAXIS: A
HOLISTIC APPROACH

> We should hunger and thirst for justice. If by justice we understand
> not only sanctity, but also the social aspect, there will be no danger
> of an angelism which would divert us from the true course. We will
> not turn our back on the social aspect. There can be no sanctity if
> nothing is done to counteract the injustices in a society which holds
> on to the institutionalized structures of sin, which deepens them and
> makes them grow.
>
> (Magana, 1974, p.93)

The contemplative and active dimensions are constitutive dimensions of the

human person and the human journey through life. However, partly due to the

prevailing cultural tendency toward dualism, the contemplative and active

dimensions are often polarized. As a result one is often pressured to claim either i)

that these two dimensions are in continual contest, or ii) that one dimension has

priority over the other. This dilemma has led spiritual masters to advise against

either/or thinking and avoid overemphazing one dimension at the expense of the

other. For example, the Dalai Lama warns that one should not rely too much on

external means of action to achieve happiness, but rather learn to nourish a strong

inner life (Dalai Lama, 1996, p.7). Conversely, Henri Nouwen, referring to the work

of Thomas Merton, pointed out that towards the end of his life, as his thought

matured, Merton cautioned against too great an emphasis upon contemplation

(Nouwen, 1991, p.24). In truth, to pursue one dimension of life to the exclusion of the other will lead to an unhealthy spirituality. A healthy spirituality must avoid polarization and foster both inner and outer dimensions for otherwise we promote "fragmentation within the person that undermines soulful living" (Beck and Kosnik, 1996, p.10). Moreover, given the global aspect of contemporary life, a healthy spirituality must include the social structures in which we live. Contemplation and work for liberation need to be integrated so as to promote an appropriate holistic spirituality for today.

The goal of this chapter is to articulate how contemplation and liberating praxis function together to form a holistic and socially responsive spirituality. I will begin by briefly exploring the polarization of contemplation and action followed by a discussion of how, paradoxically, these two dimensions, while distinct, are complementary and mutually enriching. I will then argue for a holistic approach that moves beyond polarization and propose that the dialectics of contemplation-in-action is an integrative method for fostering a spiritual life. When this dialectics is understood to incorporate the contemplative dimension within a horizon of liberating praxis, we have an appropriate method for a globally responsive and holistic spirituality for our times.

Contemplation and Action: The Polarization of Spiritual Life

Kenneth Russell has located the divorce between the contemplative and the active life in the Western Christian historical split between the spiritual and the secular. In the traditional framework, the active life, with its focus on the cares of the world, was the domain of the secular laity. The contemplative life, with its focus on the cares of the spirit, was the domain of religious and clerics (Russell, 1984, p.66). Moreover, there has been a tendency to view the contemplative life as more valuable than the active life (Palmer, 1990, p.5). When patriarchal authority augmented this approach, the result was a situation in which a healthy balance and integration between contemplation and action was difficult if not impossible to achieve.

Russell also points out that the divide was further entrenched along the line of sexual dualism in which the laity, because of their sexual activity, were barred from a deep contemplative life that was available to those celibates committed to religious life (Russell, 1984, p.69). The polarization of the contemplative and active dimensions can be traced to the predominance of dualism which permeated Western culture and which still influences our lives today.

Thomas Merton, one of the most prolific modern writers on contemplation, had to unwork this dualistic trap in his own life. In his early writings he had little appreciation for the possibility of leading a contemplative life in the secular world. He fell into using such terms as 'quasi-contemplatives' and 'masked contemplatives' (Shannon, 1981, p.22), to refer to those outside formal religious and/or contemplative communities who felt drawn to contemplative spirituality. For these, he advocated as much quiet and solitude as the demands of their life would provide (Shannon, 1981, pp.107-109). But, as Merton developed and became more cognizant of the social concerns of the world, he began to realize that one could be a full contemplative in the midst of a busy life and in the midst of social action.

> The early Merton advocated that sincere Christians flee the world and enter the solitude of the monastery. The mature Merton, on the other hand, encouraged all people to engage in contemplative prayer yet remain in the midst of the world of action. His views on contemplation took on social dimensions and became all encompassing. (Givey, 1983, p.27)

Eventually, Merton overcame the dichotomy between contemplation and action and came to see that true contemplation inevitably led to social action. Because true contemplation required an apprehension of social connections and the community in which humans find themselves, Merton believed that contemplation had to lead to social action. But, more than this, Merton believed that the most effective social action was that which was born of contemplation (Baker, 1971, pp.47-54).

The genius of Merton was that he was able to express the importance of nurturing a contemplative awareness or attitude while at the same time being aware of the demands of the world. Merton saw in contemplation the possibility of a different consciousness, one that was "free of the chaos and absurdity of the everyday world" (Givey, 1983, p.32). For Merton, this awareness required a "radical change in one's way of being and living" in which one developed an interior freedom from dependence on external rewards (Givey, 1983, p.36). This inner freedom, based on the consciousness of "a deep, underlying unity and oneness of being" formed the basis for peaceful social action (Givey, 1983, p.37).

Merton is representative of those who feel more comfortable with the contemplative side of the polarity between contemplation and action. Indeed, for Merton social action was an expression of contemplative awareness. His approach stands in continuity with the thought that one's actions flow from one's being. The limitation of Merton is that he himself was not engaged in practical social action. Except in his work as a writer, Merton remained unengaged in social and political actions in any real sense. While he wrote about social issues and social justice his primary concern was the contemplative life. There are others, Parker Palmer for example (Palmer, 1990, p.4), who have actively engaged in social action and who value the active side of the polarity over the contemplative side.

Palmer, wanting to break out of dualism, argues that spirituality must be lived where people live, "at the complicated intersection of the sacred and the secular" (Palmer, 1997, p.10). Parker offers that the monastic stress upon interiority, silence, solitude, centeredness, and balance is at odds with our modern world that values extroversion, achievement, changing structures, and bettering the world. The traditional tug-of-war between action and contemplation has given way to the active dimension taking precedence today.

> But with the Age of Exploration and the Enlightenment, with the rise of science, the Industrial Revolution, and urbanization, the rope was tugged the other way, and active life became more valued than contemplation. ... Action, not contemplation, becomes the pathway to personal virtue, to social status, and even to "salvation" for many modern men and women. (Palmer, 1990, p.6)

The contemporary fixation with action is perhaps a necessary correction to the over-emphasis upon interiority.

Palmer himself admits that his activist soul is enlivened by action much more than by the quieter side of contemplation (Palmer, 1990, p.4). He admits that too much action can often be reaction and that actions not lived in connection to "free and independent hearts" can often lead to reactive not active lives (Palmer, 1990, p.39). Despite this danger, Palmer believes that the active life has been poorly appreciated within Western spiritual traditions.

> I struggle with those parts of our spiritual tradition in which the energies of the active life are more feared than revered, pictured as wild horses to be brought under control rather than the life-giving streams that flow from the same source. (Palmer, 1990, p.7)

I agree with Palmer on this point because so much of what has been understood as spirituality in Western culture has been taught by professional religious who more often than not value the inner life as opposed to the active life.

Palmer expresses a contemporary problem concerning the need for a spirituality that values social action as a constitutive component of spiritual life, not as an outgrowth or by-product of a spiritual life which would be Merton's stance. John McGowan has traced this problem to two dominant strains in romanticism that have yet to be integrated. The spiritualist strain focuses upon consciousness, perception, and values while the realist strain focuses upon political and worldly methods of change (McGowan, 1991, p.6). Palmer is simply expressing a struggle that is deeply embedded within our culture.

In addition to Palmer others are sharing in an emerging desire for a spirituality that allows them to bring their active lives into their understanding of spirituality. Butkus has pointed out that the heart of religious education involves a commitment to both the development of the self and empowerment for prophetic communities pursuing freedom and justice (Butkus, 1989, p.572). Bosacki echoes this need when she argues for a psycho-cultural approach to transformative education that promotes both personal growth and social change "where equal focus is placed on the individual as well as the social community" (Bosacki, 1997, pp.35-38). Finally, there is a felt need for an integrated approach to spirituality that permits activists to incorporate their inner lives with their social commitments.

> Many people have turned inward, in search of an integrating center within the self that can unite committed work in the world with a deep and focused interior sense of self, incorporating not only relationship to the world and to others, but finally to God. The search for many, whether Christian or not, is for an integral way, a

spirituality sometimes called a mystical-political orientation that unites the concerns of both self and world. (Carr, 1988, p.2)

The approach of integrating contemplation and liberating praxis is a response to this felt need for a mystical-political spirituality.

Contemplation-And-Action: A Paradox That Permits Holism

Robert McAfee Brown points out that trying to bridge the work for liberation and the development of spirituality is not an easy one. Many people who pursue social justice and work for liberation of those who are disadvantaged due to structural oppression find little assistance in spiritualities that are often 'other worldly'. On the other hand, many people who pursue spirituality do not see actions to better our political and economic structures as occasions for spiritual growth. "For them, spirituality is a state of being" (Brown, 1988, p.17), rather than a way of acting.

In order to resolve this problem Brown would have us push the limits of what we understand spirituality and liberation to be. He argues that we need a radical approach that would see "spirituality and liberation as being two ways of talking about the same thing, so that there is no necessity ... of making a choice between them" (Brown, 1988, p.18). According to Brown the dichotomy between action and contemplation, spirituality and liberation, is rooted in what he calls the great fallacy of dualism. In his view, dualism serves the interests of those with power "whether political, economic, ecclesiastical, or all three – to retain that power, free from challenge" (Brown, 1988, p.30). However, if one begins to believe that "the world should not be the way it is" (Brown, 1988, p.30), that there should not be oppression, marginalization, and silencing, and that one will live "divided no more" (Palmer, 1997, p.16), then change becomes the order of the day. After this moment, one becomes ready to challenge the established order. This challenge calls for a new understanding of politics and spirituality and how these intermingle. If both spirituality and liberation were understood as the movement to "take risks, to change our priorities, to surrender our sense of self-importance" (Brown, 1988, p.112), then we would find that spirituality and liberation are two ways of talking about the same thing. In this light, both spirituality and liberation would be about getting at the root causes of injustice that prevent the world from being what it could be. In Brown's view, liberation and spirituality become terms that have reciprocal meaning and application.

> Liberation from unjust social structures means liberation for participation in creating a just society; liberation from fate means liberation for responsible action; liberation from sin and guilt means liberation for a grace-filled life... (Brown, 1988, p.123)

Brown is very aware of the need for precision in language and that the very terms 'spirituality' and 'liberation' can limit our understanding. Yet, he argues that broadening our understanding of these words to be more inclusive and radical can help to breach the divide created by the great fallacy of dualism (Brown, 1988, p.121).

In a similar vein as Brown, Palmer seeks to push the limits of our understanding of the terms contemplation and action for he recognizes the tension between these two dimensions is often due to an incomplete understanding of them. Action and contemplation are not contradictions or opposites "but poles of a great paradox that can and must be held together" (Palmer, 1990, p.7). According to Palmer, the human drive to action and contemplation is the same – the drive to be alive and to celebrate the gift of life itself (Palmer, 1990, p.15). In order to overcome any unhealthy distancing between the contemplative and active dimensions Palmer suggests that we place hyphens between the words and speak of contemplation-and-action. This would better connote the truth of human life that neither dimension can truly exist without the other.

> When we fail to hold the paradox together, when we abandon the creative tension between the two, then both ends fly apart into madness. This is what often happens to contemplation-and-action in our culture of either/or. Action flies off into frenzy – a frantic and even violent effort to impose one's will on the world, or at least to survive against the odds. Contemplation flies off into escapism – a flight from the world into a realm of false bliss. (Palmer, 1990, p.15)

Palmer argues that there are three stages in the development of contemplation-and-action: separation, alternation, and integration. The first stage wherein contemplation and action are seen as separate is followed by the second stage wherein a person alternates between active and contemplative moments. The third stage, in which a person integrates contemplation and action so that one is active when contemplating and contemplating when active results in contemplation-and-action. At this stage, the paradox of apparent opposites yields a holism wherein one realizes that "contemplation-and-action are so intertwined that features we associate with one are always found at the heart of the other" (Palmer, 1990, p.16). Palmer is able to make this claim partly because he sees contemplation and action as both connected in our desire to be fully alive. But, in addition to this he contends that in order to see the holism in the paradox we must attend to 'the hidden wholeness' that lies beyond the dualisms of our everyday life.

> Until we know the hidden wholeness, we will live in a world of dualism, of forced but false choices between being and doing that

result in action that is more frenzy or in contemplation that is mere
escape. (Palmer, 1990, p.29)

The reciprocity and complementarity between contemplation and action,
which is rooted in the human desire for life, has the effect of assisting one in
achieving a holistic approach to life. This occurs because when we act we not only
express what is within us and give shape to the world but we also receive from the
world newness that reshapes us. In this process the world and we are co-created
(Palmer, 1990, p.17). In light of this, contemplation can be a form of creative action
while action can help shape our contemplation.

Contemplation-in-Liberating Praxis: Dialectics and Integration

Matthew Fox claims that when a critical hermeneutic is not exercised within
spirituality then "the dialectic of mysticism/prophecy is ignored and creativity and
justice are relegated to forgetfulness" (Fox, 1992, p.5). Critique, then, becomes a
necessary component for spirituality today. Yet, Fox rightly argues that we must go
beyond 'mere thinking' to action rooted in critical reflection. As we do this we
should seek to link the struggle for justice with mysticism within a dialectic of action
and reflection.

> ... creation spirituality links the struggle for justice with the yearning
> for mysticism. The community's needs become the individual's needs
> and vice-versa. Prophecy, –the struggle for justice– and mysticism –
> the experience of awe, wonder and delight – form a common
> dialectic, a tension that in turn births new possibilities for community
> and individuals alike. (Fox, 1991, p.35)

Dorothy Soelle shares Fox's appreciation for critical reflection so as to
integrate, in her words, 'faith and action' (Soelle, 1974, p.3).

> As long as liberation and emancipation remain the goal, enlightened criticism is not merely optional but a necessary method. This goal is anticipated in the methodical steps of criticism – of enlightenment– even when we recognize that the dialectics of progress redefines that goal again and again. The fact that liberation has not yet been achieved is not an argument against it. (Soelle, 1974, p.4)

There is here a recognition of the fact that dialectics is progressive and open-ended. Personal and social transformation takes time. For Soelle, politics is not only a legitimate field but also the decisive sphere for the praxis of spirituality and for the pursuit of social transformation (Soelle, 1974, p.62).

Fox and Soelle are correct in calling for the importance of critical reflection for any spirituality that purports to be about politics, justice, and liberation. Their approach is consistent with Freire's idea of praxis as the dialectic of "reflection and action upon the world in order to transform it" (Freire, 1970, p.36). In the dialectical process as enunciated by Freire, action and thought must be connected together. To do otherwise is to fall into either activism or ideology (Freire, 1970, p.52). This dialectic, or dialogical method as Freire prefers to call it, is one that is oriented towards social transformation.

If liberating praxis is about keeping reflection and action together while being orientated towards liberation then we need to bring the work for justice and the experience of the mystical together. I agree with Palmer that there are moments when the two dimensions are integrated. But, unlike Palmer, I do not think these moments need to be left to chance. If we intentionally pursue an integration, a holism, then we may find that the integration of contemplation and action is more frequent than we might expect. I believe that there is an integration, a holism, in the dialectic method and that it is possible to situate this integration within the relationship between contemplation and liberating praxis. To understand the holism and integrative possibilities in dialectics let us first break down process of dialectics into its component parts.

Gadotti acknowledges the work of Freire in giving the oppressed a political voice through his use of the dialogue method. However, he argues that today dialectical pedagogy has had to build on Freire's pedagogy of dialogue by placing "the theme of power as a central theme of pedagogy" (Gadotti, 1996, p.5). Keeping in mind that theory (knowledge) and practice (action) must always be connected, Godotti has outlined four principles of dialectics to be followed in any pedagogy oriented towards change (Gadotti, 1996, p.16).

The first principle of dialectics states that "everything is related". Thus, everything is related in a coherent whole in which different parts reciprocally affect each other. Second, dialectics is about movement. Nature and society are not fixed but in continual transformation. Third, the principle of qualitative change holds that transformation takes place not through replicating the old but through the accumulation of quantitative elements. Fourth, there is the principle of contradiction and unity and struggle of opposites. Opposing forces coexist while simultaneously moving towards unity and opposition (Gadotti, 1996, pp.16-19). Applying these four principles of dialectics can help in understanding how contemplation-in-liberating praxis can be an integral and holistic spirituality.

The first principle of relatedness is consistent with my understanding of contemplation and my understanding of liberating praxis. That is, as outlined earlier, contemplation is about being attentive to the underlying unity in life, the connections that exist beyond differences, and the energy that comes from the universe itself. The contemplative orientation is very akin to the dialectical principle of everything in life being related in a coherent whole where different parts reciprocally affect each other.

This first principle is also consistent with the direction of liberating praxis. As I have argued earlier we need to keep in mind a cosmology of the earth community as a backdrop for work for social justice and liberation. Such a cosmology calls for attentiveness to relatedness, connectedness, and community between peoples, species, and all of life. Liberating praxis is a method of action and reflection with a view to moving away from divisions, separateness, and alienation to connection, relatedness, and community. This cosmological perspective which forms the backdrop for liberating praxis is consistent with the dialectical principle of relatedness.

Thus, both the contemplative and liberating praxis dimensions of human life are oriented towards the first principle of dialectics. In addition to this, the principle of relatedness applies to the two dimensions themselves. That is, contemplation and liberating praxis form a whole within which they reciprocally affect each other. Thus, contemplation impacts upon how one engages in liberating praxis and liberating praxis impacts upon how one contemplates. There are moments when, as Palmer argues, the two can operate simultaneously so one becomes a contemplative-in-liberating praxis.

The second principle of dialectics is about movement and continual transformation, which are both present in contemplation and liberating praxis. Contemplation is about being attentive to, struck by, affected by the underlying connections and unity that exists in reality. It would be incorrect to say that the connections and underlying unity are immutable. Quite the contrary. The underlying unity in the universe is dynamic. It is precisely this dynamism that creates life. It would also be incorrect to say that the underlying unity stays immutable but the one who contemplates changes. While it is true that the contemplative does change, and of necessity brings their changing consciousness to bear upon reality, it is not true that the underlying unity of life does not change. Modern physics bears this out.

> Modern physics thus pictures matter not at all as passive and inert but as being in a continuous dancing and vibrating motion whose rhythmic patterns are determined by molecular, atomic, and nuclear configurations. We have come to realize that there are no static structures in nature. There is stability, but this stability is one of dynamic balance, and the further we penetrate into matter the more we need to understand its dynamic nature to understand its patterns. (Capra, 1982, p.88)

Contemplation, with its focus on reality, yields an understanding of the continual transformation and dynamism present in all of reality.

The work of liberating praxis stands firmly on this second principle of dialectics. Freire rightly claims that persons have an 'ontological vocation' to 'act upon and transform' the world (Freire, 1970, p.12). This vocation is based on the understanding that we do not inherit a world that is static and closed, but rather inhabit a world that is dynamic and open (Freire, 1970, p.13). One who engages in liberating praxis does so with the view that one's individual choices and actions can have an impact on history, culture, and thought. When engaging in liberating praxis from a cosmological view of the earth as a community one is able to see that actions for justice in one location contribute to the emergence of a more just and humane world. Liberating praxis is therefore undertaken with an understanding that one is contributing to the ongoing transformation of society and of life itself. There is in dialectics a strong focus on the future (Gadotti, 1996, p.18), which some might dismiss as idealism, but which in practice promotes hope, an attitude absolutely necessary for engaging in liberating praxis over the long term.

Once again, this dialectical principle can be detected within the contemplative-in-liberating praxis method as well as in the two dimensions themselves. That is, in the same way that contemplation focuses on the movement and transformation continually operative in life and liberating praxis focuses on the continual transformation of nature and society, the two dimensions operate in a fashion such that they continually transform each other. Thus, that which one learns through contemplation can help to correct, support, or change how one engages in the praxis of liberation. Likewise, the learning from one's active life can correct, support, or change how one contemplates. This mutual correcting and transformation, when done within a future orientation, is what sustains this approach over the long haul for it is a method that moves between pessimism and optimism to hope.

The third principle holds that change results not from replicating old patterns but from taking incremental quantitative steps that eventually reach a threshold leading to true qualitative change. This principle is close to the heart of contemplation and action as traditionally understood and particularly applicable to contemplation-in-liberating praxis as proposed here. Contemplation-in-action is a method that comes from our religious traditions but can be moved beyond religion, which is what I am attempting to do. As such, the method, when appropriated within our contemporary concerns, can yield results that go beyond the realms of traditional religion.

Contemplation intends to bring about a change in consciousness in the individual who practices it. While one who contemplates may or may not have an initial experience of the energy, the underlying unity, and the relatedness within reality, the practice of contemplation over time normally leads to an expanded awareness of unity, relatedness, and energy. Such expansion or qualitative change is often due to small changes experienced over time as one journeys through the spiral of life.

> The journey of awareness involves a winding path along which one proceeds toward wisdom and wholeness. Yet, it is a gentle path where each winding is a complete spiral and each spiral just a winding. There are cycles of growth in a continuous process that never begins or ends. Moments of crisis and decision are growth junctures which mark a release from or death to one state of being and a growth or rebirth to the next state. (Miller, Cassie, and Drake, 1990, p.24)

The social activist who contemplates is rarely without ample crisis moments where decisions are required. Actions for social transformation very often create conflict and each moment of crisis or conflict becomes an opportunity to deepen, develop, or change one's awareness of the presence of creative energy and relatedness in the universe. Maintaining a contemplative attitude or awareness can assist in acting for liberation because in discovering points of connection within a situation, or by simply holding an attitude of expectation that connections do exist, one is better able to coordinate actions that will overcome any dehumanizing conditions.

Just as the contemplative dimension involves qualitative change so too does liberating praxis. One often engages in liberating praxis with a humble awareness of the immensity of the task. Freire himself is aware of the need for humility when engaging in the task of praxis. In his estimation "someone who cannot acknowledge himself to be as mortal as everyone else has a long way to go before he can reach the point of encounter" where transformation can take place (Freire, 1970, p.79). Social, economic, and political structures are not easy to change. On the other hand, we live in a historical time where there is plenty of evidence of the social transformation that can come about through the accumulated actions of individuals. The fall of the Iron

Curtain, the end of Apartheid in South Africa, the emergence of democracy in the Philippines, the end of racial segregation in the United States, are each examples of qualitative and historical changes that have taken place due to the cumulative actions of many people over a long period of time.

Contemplation-in-liberating praxis incorporates the third dialectical principle within its method by recognizing both in the inner moment of contemplation and the outer movement of social transformation the fact that qualitative change is the result of many smaller moments of change. Such a method intentionally seeks to continually break with the old so something new can emerge. In this sense, this spirituality is progressive and future oriented.

The fourth principle of dialectics is the principle of contradiction. Here, unity and opposition are maintained as a universal law of all material and spiritual things.

> The transformation of things is possible only because opposing forces coexist in their own interior and simultaneously move toward unity and opposition. It is this which is called "contradiction," and which is universal and inherent in all material and spiritual things. Contradiction is the essence or the fundamental law of dialectics. (Gadotti, 1996, p.19)

A contemplative is very aware of this law of contradiction. For despite momentary glimpses and a growing consciousness of the underlying unity to life, there is a parallel consciousness of the separateness and the differentiation that permeates all of life. Paradoxically, the greater the awareness of oneness the greater the awareness of pluralism. This religious paradox is akin to the dialectic principle of contradiction. The awareness of unity in difference and difference in unity permits the contemplative to value both differences in people, culture, and communities as well as areas where common ground exists between people, culture, and communities.

The dimension of liberating praxis stands too on the principle of contradiction. For while liberating praxis moves intentionally towards inclusiveness and justice for all it does not undermine individuality or the uniqueness of local contexts. It is precisely when all segments of life are harmoniously related and when every part is liberated to be fully alive that the beauty of the individual part and distinctiveness of each local culture is able to thrive. Hence, authentic unity, unlike uniformity, enables diversity to thrive and true diversity is not threatened by unity.

This contradiction between unity and opposition is one that is lived in struggle and in tension. The movement towards unity happens only because opposing forces 'coexist in their interior'. This does not mean that they necessarily coexist in their exterior. The interiority of this coexistence helps to explain why that which is common in people, things, and situations is often hidden. It is this hidden ground that enables the contemplative-in-liberating praxis to continue to seek and to act. For as Merton and Dillard know "there is a unity behind diversity, a wholeness behind the divergent forces of life" (Palmer, 1990, p.30). It is this hidden ground that also accounts for why contemplation and action, while interdependent and mutually beneficial, are often lived in tension, for from the tension creativity and life flow.

There is, then, a healthy holistic dynamic that takes place in the dialectic between contemplation and liberating praxis. The focus on relatedness and connection, the conviction that transformation is necessary and possible, the experience that qualitative personal and social change does take place over time, and the acceptance of the creative tension that lies in the contradictory pull of unity and differentiation: all these combine to make contemplation-in-liberating praxis a vibrant and creative spiritual approach to life. Dialectics permits us to move beyond any polarization of contemplation and liberating praxis and even beyond contemplation-and-liberating praxis where periodically the alternating dimensions merge. Dialectics allows for a more comprehensive understanding of how contemplation and liberating praxis interconnect to such an extent that contemplation-in-liberating praxis becomes the model to pursue for it moves far beyond any tendency to fall into any false dualism that would promote either disengaged spiritualism or dispirited activism.

Conclusion

Jungian analysts Woodman and Dickson have pointed to the connection between the personal and the social from a psychological perspective. "It is only by recognizing and healing the dualities that exist in ourselves that we can come to a true sense of interdependence with the rest of creation" (Woodman and Dickson, 1996, p.53). While one does not have to accept their premise that the starting point must be with the personal self, I do think that they are correct in making the connection between the personal and the social. The outer constructs of the world around us are often mirrored within our inner selves. The dualism that exists 'out there' also exist 'in me'. The structures that divide and oppress are often appropriated within the self. Or as Freire says, "the oppressed suffer from the duality which has established itself in their innermost being" (Freire, 1970, p.32).

Concurrent with the growing awareness of the need to free the inner person of internalized dualism there is also a growing awareness that our world is more interdependent than we ever imagined. As this consciousness grows we are coming to see that "the particular "I" cannot have justice unless the other "I" has justice – that others cannot have clean water to drink unless I respect the earth" (Woodman and Dickson, 1996, p.54). What is required is a project in which both personal well being and global well being are mutually promoted.

Contemplation-in-liberating praxis is about such a project for in integrating the two dimensions of contemplation and social action, inner and outer, personal and social, we are able to pursue a course that cares for both the self and the other simultaneously. The holism contained within a dialectics of contemplation-in-liberating praxis ensures that, over time, a healthier world for all can be created and sustained. Because of this contemplation-in-liberating praxis is an appropriate method for spiritual education for our world today.

Still, it is one thing to clarify a method. It is another thing to apply it. For as Robert McAfee Brown warns, "the recovery of the unity of spirituality and liberation must be exhibited in the day-to-day events of human lives rather than in the line-to-line sentences of human books" (Brown, 1988, p.135). The questions now become: How do we educate for contemplation-in-liberating praxis? Where can we do this? Who can teach this method? These are the concerns for the next chapter.

CHAPTER FIVE

SOME PEDAGOGICAL CONSIDERATIONS FOR CONTEMPLATION-IN-LIBERATING PRAXIS

> Every educator – and I use the term in its widest sense – should
> constantly ask himself whether he is actually fulfilling his teachings
> in his own person and in his own life, to the best of his knowledge
> and with a clear conscience. Psychotherapy has taught us that in the
> final reckoning it is not knowledge, not technical skill, that has a
> curative effect, but the personality of the doctor. And it is the same
> with education: it presupposes self-education. (Jung, 1981,p.140)

Thus far I have argued for contemplation-in-liberating praxis as an appropriate method for spiritual education today. In integrating 'wonderstruck beholding' and liberating praxis within a dialectical holism I am simply broadening the traditional approach of contemplation-in-action to address the concerns of our day. Such an approach is dynamic, creative, and life giving and may hold some currency for educators today.

The concern of this chapter is with the practical issues of how to actually educate for contemplation-in-liberating praxis. An appeal to traditional spiritual practices, contemporary thinkers on spiritual education, and the praxis methods from both religious and secular sources will help to expedite this task. I shall begin with a brief discussion of the relationship between the individual and community simply because spiritual education, like all education, involves a marriage of both the personal and the social. I will then discuss some strategies for educating for the contemplative dimension and follow this with some strategies for educating for liberating praxis. The role and responsibilities of the teacher and the relationship between teacher and student will be briefly explored. One cannot discuss the area of spirituality without addressing concerns of phase theorists and developmentalists. As such, I will discuss how I see developmental approaches fitting within the dialectical method of contemplation-in-liberating praxis I am proposing. Finally, the question of what are the most appropriate and effective locations for education for contemplation-in-liberating praxis will be addressed.

The Person in Community

It is prudent, lest one misunderstand the discussion in this chapter as falling back into an unhealthy promotion of privatism and individualism, to say something about community. I am in agreement with those who contend that we become persons in and through our relationship with others (Del Prete, 1990, p.32). Bellah and his colleagues pointed out the limits of individualism in American society and argued that we can only fully be individuals within communities.

> We find ourselves not independently of other people and institutions but through them. We never get to the bottom of our selves on our own. We discover who we are face to face and side by side with others in work, love, and learning. All of our activity goes on in relationships, groups, associations, and communities ordered by institutional structures and interpreted by cultural patterns of meaning. Our individualism is itself one such pattern. And the positive side of our individualism, our sense of dignity, worth, and moral autonomy of the individual, is dependent in a thousand ways on a social, cultural, and institutional context that keeps us afloat when we cannot very well describe it. (Bellah et. al., 1986, p.84).

It is true that the society and community in which one lives contributes to one's identity. It is also true that society and community contribute to one's spirituality.

As such, while we can understand that spirituality is personal, it is also "radically communitarian" (Fox, 1991, p.12).

Now, it is difficult in North America to appreciate the communal nature of spirituality. In other parts of the world where community takes precedence over the individual, it is easier to understand spirituality as communal. It was the concern for communal spirituality that led Gustavo Gutierrez, when writing about the Latin American experience, to say that "we are talking here about the journey of an entire people, not of isolated individuals" (Gutierrez, 1985, p.72). For Gutierrez the experience of the poor in Latin America points to spirituality being a communal enterprise (Gutierrez, 1985, p.137).

But, as Bellah and his colleagues have pointed out, although community is an integral part of spiritual development in North America, we tend not to appreciate this because we so highly prize the individual. We do not have a well-articulated 'public spirituality' that Berry suggests we need. My point in bringing up this concern regarding the communal and the individual is to acknowledge that I do recognize that the community contributes to spirituality as personally lived. To educate for contemplation-in-liberating praxis one needs to continually bear this in mind.

We must also recognize that not only does the community form the individual but the individual contributes to the formation of the community.

> If now we turn to the other pole, community, we meet a paradox: the becoming of individuals is the very creation of community. It is not enough to say that community is necessary for the formation and education of individuals. True as that is, it does not go deep enough. To do so one has to say that the very achievement of the freedom and unique individuality of each person is identical with the achievement of community. (Davis, 1987, p.39)

Thus, as persons become fully actualized and individualized they contribute to the on-going creation of the community or communities in which they are located. Authentic communities promote personhood and authentic persons promote communities.

Essentially, there is a dialectic between persons and communities. According to Palmer, persons contribute to communities by means of projection while communities contribute to persons by means of conditioning (Palmer, 1983, p.12). While we should be careful not to push the notions of projection and conditioning to extremes, these do point to a process whereby not only can community create the context and conditions for contemplation-in-liberating praxis but the persons who engage in this method can contribute to the creation of the communal and public spirituality.

To promote both personal and communal/public spirituality we need to understand that the community and the individual are in a process of dialogue. The outer world of community can help to provide meaning for our personal experiences. Stories, symbols, rituals, codes, and rules can help to shape our experiences (Peterson, 1992, pp.15-37). At the same time, our personal experiences can be brought to bear upon the stories, symbols, rituals, codes and rules that shape our public life. In this way, individual experiences shape the character of the community. The individual is given meaning by the community and the community is given meaning by the individual. This dialogue is open-ended, on going, dynamic, and supportive.

The strategies that follow, while immediately available for personal use, have potential to contribute to community. Some are more easily appropriated as communal actions, while others will benefit the community to the extent that the persons who practice them contribute to the community. Thus, the pedagogical concerns raised here will continually be trying to break through the dualism between individualism and community which is rooted deeply within our personal psyche and collective consciousness.

Strategies for Facilitating Contemplation

I have argued in this study that contemplation involves a wonderstruck beholding of the underlying oneness in the universe and the interconnectivity and relatedness of life. This awareness involves a "long, loving look at the real" (Burghardt, 1984, p.14), "wonderstruck thinking" (Buchmann, 1989, p.36), wonder (Cavalletti, 1983, p.140), and a feeling of being "at-one-with" reality (Russell, 1987, p.196). Moreover, contemplation does not negate pluralism but rather sees diversity as the result of the creative energy within the universe.

The capacity to contemplate is innate to the human person. However, like any human capacity, it needs to be educated. As such, certain strategies, conditions, and tools can be used to help facilitate the development of the contemplative dimension. A few of these are as follows.

i) **Silence and Solitude**

Contemplatives who engage in political action need to nurture their inner life and be attentive to their awareness of self and the world around them. Silence and solitude can assist in such awareness because while alone in silence we are challenged to move beyond excessive rationalism to seek the truth that lies within the self and in reality. "In silence, the rational mind wearies of seeking truth by main force and humbles itself to the truth that seeks us." (Palmer, 1983, p.117) One enters into solitude and silence so as to listen to one's inner self and to one's interior movements and motivations. Our emotions, imaginations, and intentions have a direct impact upon not only how we perceive the world, but also how we act in it. As such, solitude permits the contemplative the opportunity to examine his or her inner life so that the inner person engaging in the political action is acting in fidelity to one's truest self. The more one attends to the various components of one's inner life and seeks to arrive at a contemplative acceptance of the often divergent elements, the more one is able to 'sense' the underlying unity that exists in all of reality.

Through solitude and periods of silence a contemplative is able to clarify their inner life and connect to their inner source of life. Merton saw the need for giving attention to the person of the activist and being attentive to the ground of being within the self as well as outside the self (Del Prete, 1990, p.111).

> Merton was concerned not so much with "action" as with the basis of action; not so much with the activists' central question, "What can we do to most effectively achieve our goals?" as with the contemplative's "Who are we who are acting?". (Del Prete, 1990, p.110)

I agree with Merton on the need for attention to the person of the activist because it has been my observation that the integrity of a person has as much impact as their message or their action.

Taking time for solitude and silence is necessary for the clarification of one's motivations and desires regarding the liberating action one is engaging in or planning to engage in. But solitude and silence cannot be divorced from community and society and most definitely should not be seen as ends in themselves (Kamperindis, 1992, p.14). In fact, into solitude and silence the contemplative brings the concerns of the world and the community and acts as a sort of "mediator in the social issues preoccupying his community" (Kamperindis, 1992, p.16). The contemplative brings the works of liberating praxis, as well as the inner work of interiority, into the moments of silence and solitude so that the concerns of the active life are attended to as well as the more reflective and contemplative life.

Merton advised that those seeking contemplation should deliberately create a lifestyle that promoted solitude and was less preoccupied with work and concerns of the world (Shannon, 1981, pp.107-108). However, his focus was more on promoting a monastic spirituality, rather than the contemplation-in-liberating praxis method I am proposing. Consequently, his advice holds limited currency for those engaged in social and political actions. Moments of silence and solitude must be found in the midst of life. Certainly, one can withdraw from the demands of one's life for short periods and seek the silence and solitude necessary for inner renewal. But, I think we need to find those quiet moments in our daily life in which we embrace the silence permitted us and the solitude available to us. My daily life and responsibilities of family, friends, work, and political action are the context where I ultimately must live my solitude and silence. Gutierrez argues along this line when he holds that community is the location for solitude.

> There is, however, no question here of two stages: first solitude and then community. Rather, it is within community that one experiences solitude. (Gutierrez, 1985, p.132)

Contemplative practice, then, is not at odds with community and/or the work of social action. It is integral to both community and to liberating praxis. The more we behold the reality around us, the better prepared we are to engage in communal work of transformation.

ii) Meditation

If contemplation is about seeing reality as it is, as with 'walking with the camera lens open' (Dillard, 1988, p.31), or living with a 'receptive mode of consciousness' (Miller, 1993, p.46), then we need to learn to let down the cognitive barriers that separate us from reality. Meditation, as "the practice, the art of letting down the barriers" (Kelsey, 1976, p.37), can assist in contemplation.

Miller sees the active mode of consciousness as concerned with our exterior life while the receptive mode is used to see and listen to the world around us and within us. Miller suggests using mantras, movement meditations, breath meditations, and visual meditation to bring calm and order to life. The onus is on the individual to follow a meditative form that best suits them (Miller, 1993, pp.54-59). Miller is correct that some form of meditative practice is important for nurturing one's inner life.

Meditation is helpful in contemplation as well. While contemplation does involve a concern for inner peace and tranquillity, the key concern is awareness of the underlying unity in life. Through meditation on elemental symbols such as fire, light, and water, a contemplative can focus their attention, quieten their inner discourse, and achieve a level of inner openness to reality so that the underlying unity and interconnectivity can be discovered.

Still, the contemplative who engages in liberating praxis does not meditate in a vacuum. Social and political concerns cannot be left out of meditation. Bringing the concerns of the world into meditative practice can heighten our capacity to see connections and solutions in difficult situations. Jose Magana has attempted to do this with his reworking of the Ignatian Exercise (1974). The Ignatian Exercise were compiled by St. Ignatius of Loyola and involved the use of active imagination and guided meditation to assist a person in meditation. Magana has reworked the

Exercises to include social and political realities within active imagination. In my own work I have at times invited students to take part in guided imagination exercises that include concerns such as poverty and racism and I have found if very effective. Students find that both their imagination and compassion are activated during these moments. This is the direction which contemplatives engaged in liberating praxis would want to go.

iii) Emotions and Body

If contemplation is more a way of 'sensing' reality than a cognitive approach to reality then it must include more than our rational faculties. It must include our emotional life and care of our body. Beck and Kosnik, in wanting to move away from our Western mistrust of the emotions, have argued that we need to attend to our emotional life not only because of the motivational value of emotions (Beck and Kosnik, 1995, p.162), but also because emotions help to promote our well-being.

> It is not enough to experience emotions. We must also acknowledge our emotions, accept them by and large, and express them as appropriate. If we do not admit that we have emotions such as pleasure, affection, desire, fear, anger, pain, they will do harm in our lives .... and we will not be able to harness their positive directions and energies. (Beck and Kosnik, 1995, pp.162-163)

It is true that we need to pay more attention to the role of the emotions in education. Noddings has called for attentiveness to emotions and affectivity (Noddings, 1986, pp.132-147), while Palmer has argued that teachers need to permit space for emotions to live (Palmer, 1983, p.83).

It is important to heed our emotions because our feelings are related to what is valuable in our lives (Lonergan, 1972, pp.30-32). We respond at an affective level when what we hold as valuable is promoted or demoted. Contemplation, as wonderstruck beholding of reality, "engages the emotions" (Buchmann, 1989, p.47), and calls forth feelings of joy, awe, peace, and happiness. As such, contemplation can give us energy and motivation to live. When we contemplate and see reality as fundamentally connected we can be filled with positive emotions that can fuel our desire and passion to promote life and well-being for all in our world.

It is important to attend to emotions not only because of their positive utility but also because emotions, if blocked or suppressed, can inhibit our contemplative and active lives. For contemplatives engaged in social action it is particularly important to listen to their emotions because otherwise the danger is burnout.

> The care of others starts to be real work. A growing burden of personal responsibility leads to exhaustion and frustration. We feel as if we're putting out more than we're getting back. ... As our heart begins to close down, joy and inspiration give way to apathy and resignation. There arises a range of emotions and responses we've come to call burnout. (Ram Dass, 1985, pp.184-185)

Feelings of anger, resentment, jealousy, and fatigue can signal an unhealthy engagement that creates an imbalance between contemplation and action. So, we need to listen to our emotions for they will yield important information about ourselves (Moore, 1992, pp.137-138).

Within this discussion of emotions a word about anger and 'resentment' is necessary. Very often social activists are accused of being motivated by anger, bitterness, and resentment. Activists need to be aware of the distinction between justifiable anger and 'resentment'. Justifiable anger is an anger proportionally related to the injustice faced and is ultimately creative. It is the emotion which leads to what Brueggemann calls, "prophetic energizing" (Brueggemann, 1978, pp.62-79).

'Resentiment', on the other hand, is an attitude of continually belittling and is ultimately destructive (Lonergan, 1972, p.33). There is room within contemplation-in-liberating praxis for justifiable anger, but any hint of 'resentiment' essentially undermines this direction.

Finally, intimately connected to listening to our emotions is the need to listen to our body for our body often holds information about our life.

> If we could learn to listen to our bodies, and realize they are giving us information we need to know via the symptoms, the situation might improve. Very often it is just that; our body is telling us something because we have not been open to hearing it in any other way. (Sanford, 1977, p.31)

I mean here not only the awareness that our body holds different centers of energy or chackras (Woodman and Dickson, 1996, pp.58-61), although this is important for personal awareness. We must also include an awareness of our physical body and its needs as we enter into contemplation. Also, I believe we need to include a respectful listening to our body about what it might tell us about our practical engagement in liberating praxis. The work of liberation can bring joy and hardship and these need to be given room to live in the contemplative life. Might I suggest dance and movement to express joy, celebration, and life and tears to express sorrow, disappointment and discouragement? Our body can be a vehicle for self-expression and such self-expression can contribute to the contemplative awareness of the underlying unity within the universe.

iv) Family, Friends, and Community

If contemplation is lived within community and if community provides the context for contemplation, then relationships are important for contemplation. Too often those involved in social justice tend to become bitter, disillusioned, and destructive. We tend to become more ideological, driven, and hard rather than open, creative, and responsive. An antidote to this danger, in addition to silence, solitude, meditation, and attention to body and emotions, is to develop and maintain good friendships.

> Only friendship can save us. Loving, challenging friends who can melt our bitterness and free us from the need to be angry are as critical within the spiritual life as are prayer and social justice. To neglect friendship is to court bitterness and perversion. (Rolheiser, 1991, p.29)

True friends call forth the best in us and it is the best in us that must be brought forward when we contemplate. Friends support us not only in our contemplation but also in our work for liberation. Without their support "we will be unable to be of much help to people further afield" (Beck, 1993, p.66). Hence, time must be allotted for nurturing friendships and support of family members, for these are part of the community that holds us while we contemplate. We must also find support in communities of like-minded others who value contemplation and its social and political ramifications.

v) Read, Play, and Celebrate

Walter Burghardt advises that contemplatives play, celebrate, and read. He argues that a sense of 'play' is close to the contemplative attitude of awe and creativity. One ought to enter into the world with a 'playful' attitude, open to surprises, without any attempt to control or possess the world (Burghardt, 1984, pp.9-10). A contemplative approach to reality recognizes that the whole universe is a 'play ground' where paradoxes can startle and inspire us.

> To attempt to live without humor, without awareness of paradox all
> around us and within us, without the ability to laugh even and
> especially at ourselves is to contradict the universe itself. Too much
> sobriety violates the laws of nature. What Eckhart calls "unself-
> consciousness" is often expressed in our ability to let go with cosmic
> laughter; it is a necessary dimension to common survival and
> therefore to our ethics. (Fox, 1991, p.52)

When we play we give room for our creative impulses to live. When we contemplate
we see the creativity that lies within all of life and we rejoice in it.

Celebration is connected to play for it is often the way communities play.
That is, when family, friends, or community seek to celebrate an event, there is often
unleashed a sense of joy, excitement, and laughter. Celebrations are important
because "people cannot live gracefully or peacefully, joyfully or justly, without
celebration in their lives, without awe" (Fox, 1991, p.29). In entering into
celebrations, the contemplative is reminded that the creative impulse of the world is
present in the community that gathers. This creativity is alive in the community and
can, if not forced or controlled, be a source of inspiration and support for
contemplative practice. With regard to the political realm, because social and
political action can often be difficult, it is all the more important that celebration be
encouraged. When a community can continue to celebrate and a person continue to
contemplate despite the injustices that exist around them, then a hope that can sustain
long term action is able to live.

Finally, Burghardt suggests that contemplatives read the works of
"remarkable men and women who have themselves looked long and loving at the
real" (Burghardt, 1984, p.10). He suggests Nikos Kazantzakis, Dag Hammarskjold,
Gandhi, Thoreau, Merton, Teresa of Avila, Teilhard de Chardin, and others. I would
suggest people like Dorothy Day, Nelson Mandela, the Berrigan brothers and others

who have deliberately sought to integrate the area of political action within their spiritual practice. Through meditative reading we can find support for our contemplative life.

The above are a few strategies for developing a contemplative approach to life and nurturing the awareness of all of life as connected. These strategies are intended to facilitate the experience of oneness, wonder, and awe that accompanies contemplative experience. This experience is decisive for a spirituality oriented towards liberation for it provides the conviction, the groundedness, and the energy so necessary to sustain one in the pursuit of justice.

Strategies for Facilitating Liberating Praxis

Education for the active dimension that is focused on liberating praxis as the complement to contemplation within the method of contemplation-in-action requires a pedagogy that "makes the pedagogical more political and the political more pedagogical" (Giroux, 1988, p.127). As such, the strategies for facilitating liberating praxis intentionally bring structural and political questions into the active dimension of spirituality. The following strategies can best be appreciated if one remembers that the contemplative dimension should be kept in continual dialogue with the actions intended for social transformation.

i) Solidarity

The first step in liberating praxis can be summarized by the statement that "if you want to know what is being done here, you should be here" (Evans and Dallaire, 1989, p.27). This was a statement made by a woman who lived in a public housing project where I worked for several years as an ecumenical chaplain. Made at an annual general meeting it had the effect of challenging the various stakeholders who were connected to the chaplaincy to become more personally involved in the housing project itself. The challenge was taken up and the result was the birth of a community chaplaincy that continues to this day.

If social and political transformation is brought about through transformative communities then it is imperative that individuals who wish to act for liberation be engaged in a concrete community. Any attempt to problematize or conceptualize around concerns of justice "without ever actually engaging humans, whatever the issues, alienates and dehumanizes" (Street, 1988, p.231). Education for liberation cannot be founded upon abstraction or without attention to the people in the context. The ultimate power behind liberating praxis is that it is built upon relationships and is concerned about bettering the lives of actual people.

The first step, then, is to locate oneself within the community. This moment of location is not the moment for action. It a moment is which one needs to be contemplative in that one needs to be open and attentive and adopt a listening stance. All effective involvement for justice stems from solidarity. 'Being there' permits time for "listening to the experience of the poor, the marginalized, the oppressed in our society" (De Roo, 1991, p.39). From this listening stance we are able to get a realistic grasp of how social and political issues actually impact upon specific persons. This awareness creates the bedrock for action and reflection.

ii) Awareness Through Dialogue

Freire argues that the human person, no matter how uneducated in a formal sense, has the innate capacity to critique the world. This capacity for critique is best actualized through dialogue with others. Through dialogue people can identify the issues operative in their world and thereby can gain power over those issues. This power is the power of knowledge and it provides the basis for the freedom to act.

Through the awareness that emerges from dialogue persons take control of their history and see themselves as subjects not objects of history. Awareness through dialogue is the crucible of change (Freire, 1970, pp.12-15).

The movement towards awareness is the movement of conscientization. "Conscientization can be defined as the process in which persons achieve a deepening awareness, both of the socio-cultural reality that shapes their lives and their capacity to transform that reality" (Schipani, 1984, p.ix). Conscientization, achieved through dialogue, involves the exploration of three areas.

First is the exploration of the social and political structures that impact upon the people concerned. This involves a critical analysis of the "economic, political, and social structures that cause human suffering" (De Roo, 1991, p.39). An exploration of the 'thematic universe' can assist in this analysis. A thematic universe is the term Freire uses to describe the complex of themes (each representing ideas, values, hopes, and challenges) which vary from one location to the next (Schipani, 1984, p.4). For example, the Canadian thematic universe includes the complex of capitalism, colonialism, individualism, democracy, and social welfare. An examination of the thematic universe involves an exploration of the generative themes, that is, how the general themes are lived in the particular context (Schipani, 1984, p.4), (e.g. how low income Canadians fare in the global economy), and of the limit situations present in society (e.g. how poor Canadians are systemically marginalized from the benefits of the global economy). The study of the social and political structures involves not only themes but also how participants perceive those themes. This leads to the second area of exploration that concerns internalization.

Freire argues that what often inhibits people who are oppressed from working for liberation is that they have internalized the world as modeled by the oppressors. For Freire it is not so much that the oppressed believe the myths propagated to continue oppression (e.g. welfare recipients are lazy) but that they fear that should they ever acquire power they too would oppress others. Because of this internalization the oppressed must become conscious that by allowing themselves to be 'hosts' of oppression, they permit oppression to continue. The key to breaking with oppression is the awareness that both the oppressed and the oppressor are participants in and suffer from oppression. For example, some feminists have rightly argued that oppressors victimize themselves through their oppressive tactics. Hence, men are unable to fully become men if their status is dependent upon dominating women. Freire is correct in pointing out how victims of oppression can often internalize the myths used to legitimate oppression. He is also correct in pointing out the importance of identifying the impact which oppressive myths have on those who benefit from structural injustice. Uncovering how injustice hurts both oppressed and oppressor is key to engaging oppressors in transformative change. This possibility does exist, but sadly, it does not exist often.

The third area for dialogue for conscientization is the exploration of possibilities for liberation. A pedagogy for liberating praxis must not only include socio-political critique but also visioning for social justice. "For radical pedagogy to become a viable political project, it has to develop a discourse that combines the language of critique with the language of possibility" (Freire in Giroux, 1988, p.xxxii). What is required, then, is not only a dismantling of the dominant consciousness that is operative in the community, a dismantling aided by critical dialogue, but also the offering of alternatives that can be pursued. As Bruegemann would argue (Bruegemann, 1978, pp.28-43), we need to move from a royal consciousness to an alternative consciousness. Hence, we need to move from accepting things as they are to embracing an alternative vision of how things could be.

130

The cosmological perspective of the earth as a community of interrelated parts can give rise to such an alternative consciousness. The more we see specific injustices as connected to other injustices; the more we seek to overcome these injustices by building communities committed to change; the more we encourage dialogue between different groups and pursue a worldview that upholds all species as valuable and in need of care, the better we will be able to pursue liberation. Here a contemplative approach can be helpful. The contemplative awareness and openness to the underlying connections in all of reality can orient one to better see the connections that are required within a cosmological perspective. The contemplative's development of the skills of attentiveness, creativity, and playfulness can all be brought to bear when exploring the possibilities of alternative ways of organizing our world to meet concrete needs.

iii) Action

Becoming aware of the causes of injustice, how these can be internalized, and what alternatives are possible must be followed by action. It is in engaging in actions for liberation that we bring about change for without action our consciousness raising is futile. In fact, the decisive moment in liberating praxis is the moment of action (Fox, 1991, p.75).

Ideally, the task of action is taken up by both oppressor and oppressed. When both oppressors and oppressed become conscious of the sources of injustices and are able to see an alternative way, then they may feel obligated to promote actions that move in the direction of the alternative. To do otherwise is, in Freire's view, "a farce" (Freire, 1970, p.35). Baum would go further and claim that non-participation in transforming unjust structures after one has become conscious of those structures results in social sin (Baum, 1975, pp.201-202). More often than not, though, actions for change usually come from individuals and communities of activists who are themselves marginalized from privilege and status.

Action for liberation is best undertaken in community. While there is no doubt that individuals can impact upon social, economic, and political structures, more often than not it is the power of community that brings about change. Communities tend to be able to generate more resources and strategies than one individual. Communities oriented towards liberation will attend to the needs of different members of the community so that no individual is sacrificed in the quest for liberation.

As such, there is a need for communities to brainstorm possible alternative ways of organizing, evaluate their options, and make judgments about the path to be taken. Once decisions have been made, then the community needs to implement the decisions. Examples of communal actions from a Canadian perspective would include: civil protest, worker cooperatives, corporate lobbying, community kitchens, pay equity, letter writing campaigns, boycotts, and supporting alternative methods of food production.

iv) Reflection on Action

The praxis method keeps action and reflection together in a constant dialogue. Hence, activists need to take time to reflect upon their actions. This reflection can either follow specific actions or take place concurrently with the action. Since the most effective action is communal action it stands that the best reflection will to be a communal experience. Such reflection requires dialogue between participants, listening to others, openness to challenge and collaboration (Willets, 1995, p.10).

> The third task in the praxis model is reflection on practice. Reflective practice means being at work in the world, practicing, reflecting on the results of one's practice, making decisions about how to modify or alter one's practice in order to increase one's effectiveness, deciding whether and what additional information may be needed, and engaging again in practice. The cycle of action is continuous: reflecting, acting, and reflecting again. (Willet, 1995, p.11)

Quite obviously, when a community does the reflection on praxis it will involve a great deal more time than if engaged in on an individual basis. However, taking the time to reflect upon the efficacy of the actions a community has chosen is essential. Through a revisitation of the questions regarding structures of injustice, the cosmology of the earth as a community, and the results of the actions taken, those seeking a transformed world can re-assess, correct, or modify their actions. On-going reflection is essential precisely because, very often, bringing about social and political change can be a long project. If the moment of reflection on praxis was undertaken while removed from the action itself, then there is a need to return to the action with the fruits of reflection to be brought to the action.

v) Embracing Contemplative Moments

Just as we can bring social and political concerns into our contemplation, we can also bring our contemplation into our work of liberating praxis. There are moments during the entire process of liberating praxis in which we can embrace contemplative moments. I have already alluded to the contemplative attitude of openness and listening that can be useful in 'being there', immersed in a community. Contemplating things as they are and the underlying unity in reality can assist in seeing the needs of the community. The non-attachment approach of contemplation can help create a climate in which the community can open up to transformative possibilities.

Moreover, during the phase of conscientization, the contemplative approach of seeking connections, unity, and energy can provide an additional dimension. The analytical moment tends towards dissection, discrimination and judgment. This is a necessary requirement. However, the contemplative attentiveness to unity and connections can help to prevent any excessive analysis or judgment and provide for a more holistic analysis.

Moments of silence, meditation, play, and celebration can assist in the deconstruction of the dominant consciousness and the entertainment of an alternative consciousness. Allowing for solitude can provide the opportunity for individuals within a community to pause and reflect in a deeper way about how the actions for liberation impact upon individuals and the community. When a community allows for a 'contemplative pause' it allows for sober second thought.

Moreover, because contemplation is focused on the dynamism of the present moment it can provide the basis for hope, which can sustain liberating praxis. How essential it is for activists to be alive and hopeful as they engage in their work for change. Having a sense of the importance of the life energy permeating each moment can help to ward off disappointment, disillusionment, and frustration. It can help to provide a balance and a perspective to the often difficult task of liberation.

Finally, taking moments to contemplate while one is engaging in political action can help focus one on the task at hand. It can help strengthen one's resolve and commitment. It can help keep a person rooted in their best self because the contemplative is concerned with not only the action being taken, but also who the person is who engages in the action. Ultimately, because individuals on-goingly create communities, those communities opting to pursue socio-political liberation will find great support in promoting contemplation.

The strategies for facilitating liberating praxis are best learned through participation. Essentially, one must jump in, 'feet first', and engage in the process of solidarity, awareness, action, reflection, and contemplation. Through experience and with others liberating praxis can be an effective method for engaging one's spiritual life in the work of liberation.

The Role of the Teacher and The Relationship with Students

In order to teach contemplation-in-liberating praxis as a spirituality a teacher must be a contemplative-in-liberating praxis. A teacher who pursues their own contemplative dimension while being attentive to the active life of socio-political transformation is the best model for this spiritual practice. A teacher of this spirituality will appreciate and be able to speak about the underlying connections that exist in reality and the energy that permeates this reality. They will be engaged in and fluent in the practices that aid in contemplative awareness: silence, solitude, meditation, emotions, body, relationships, celebration, and reading. Jack Miller has mapped out the importance of teachers working with various techniques to facilitate their own inner life so that they can be better reflective practitioners for their students (Miller, 1994, pp.51-84).

Moreover, such teachers will be able to connect their contemplative practice with their praxis for liberation. Teachers of this spirituality will also be engaged in liberating praxis, seeing their role as public intellectuals to be one of transforming society (Giroux, 1988, pp.100-101). They will engage in action for justice, be reflective about this engagement, and seek to bring their praxis to their contemplation. They will be transformative intellectuals seeking to "educate students to be active, critical citizens" (Giroux, 1988, p.127). But, more than being intellectuals, teachers linking contemplation and social justice will be exercising a prophetic role. "The prophet is one who sees people and their situations as they really are, who feels intimately the things that are going on around him or her and who refuses simply to let them continue." (Hansen, 1991, p.206)

The integration of contemplation, seeing reality as it is, and liberating praxis, refusing to let injustice continue, is the way of prophecy. Hence, the teacher who acts as a role model for integrating contemplation and liberation will be a radical, a transformative and public intellectual, and a prophet. They will teach for an alternative "way of being in the world" (Palmer, 1983, p.30).

Obviously, these teachers will not be seeking to conserve the status quo through engaging in 'banking' or 'narrative' education whereby teachers deposit knowledge into students who receive and store the data for possible future use (Freire, 1970, p.58). Conservative pedagogies simply serve to indoctrinate students into the rules and values of society (Giroux, 1988, p.34), and are in no way intended to bring about transformation. Contemplatives-in-liberating praxis, with their focus on transforming society, will opt for non-indoctrination and adopt critique rather than socialization. They will also move beyond the reform stance of liberal educators who, thinking they are critical of society, are too caught in the myths of progress through social melioration, meritocracy, professionalism, and traditional schooling for their work to be truly radical (Giroux, 1988, p.36). Teachers who embrace contemplation-in-liberating praxis will be radicals in the sense that they will wish to go to the roots of problems of social injustice. Going to the root will necessitate a return to the core of our personal and social problems and seeking to work through the issues with the holistic approach found in contemplation-in-liberation.

The teacher as contemplative-in-liberating praxis must see the relationship with students as a partnership in pursuit of contemplation and reflective actions that liberate. For this partnership to be effective, the teacher must be in 'communion' (Freire, 1970, p.47), in 'solidarity' (Giroux, 1988, p.217), with his or her students. This will happen to the extent that the relationship between teacher and student is marked by a democratic practice where power is shared and owned by both participants in the learning process.

The dialectic found in the method of contemplation-in-action will be found as well in the relationship between the teacher and student. There will be a back and forth dialogue between teacher and student as they explore contemplation and liberating action together. A new kind of relationship will emerge, one marked by mutuality and respect. "Through dialogue, the teacher-of-the-students and the students-of-the-teacher cease to exist and a new term emerges: teacher-students with students-teacher." (Freire, 1970, p.67) In this new relationship both teacher and students will know themselves to be continually 'on the way' to contemplating reality and active contributors to a transformed and more just world. Where Giroux argues that both teacher and student need to be seen as transformative intellectuals I argue that both teacher and students need to be seen as contemplatives-in-liberating praxis. As such, students will reveal what they have learned through their contemplative practice and through their reflective actions for liberation in the same way as the teacher will. This exchange will assist in making the learning dynamic and empowering.

This dialogical and democratic relationship between teacher and student will not negate differences, for their will be differences due to experience, age, perspective, and responsibilities. While teachers will have their own perspective in some areas students will have more experience, skill, and insight than the teacher.

However, these differences will simply add to the dynamism of the dialogue between student and teacher and between these contemplatives-in-liberating praxis and the world in which they live.

Maintaining the dialogue between teacher and student requires a profound love for the world, for people, and for society. Without love, which I understand here to be respect and high regard for the other, there can be no true dialogue. This spiritual method stands upon the capacity of teachers and students to love not only themselves but also their world. This method also requires humility in the hearts of those who participate in the educational dialogue so that authentic communication can take place. Still, the dialogue requires a third element, a faith in the human capacity to create history. Without a faith in this capacity, a person is unable to see possibilities for creative change. Moreover, hope must be present for true dialogue to occur because hope opens us to the future. Hope is an essential condition for those who seek to engage in liberating works. Finally, true dialogue depends upon critical thinking for this permits one to judge the present with a view of humanizing society. These attributes (love, humility, faith in history, hope, and critical thinking) are essential preconditions for true dialogue according to Freire (Freire, 1970, pp.75-62). For true dialogue to take place between the teacher and students of contemplation and action I would add the capacity to listen to silence, to embrace solitude, to meditate, to play, and to care for one's emotional and physical needs. When all these elements are included within the moments of learning, then a context is created whereby education for contemplation-in-liberating praxis can be effective and fruitful.

Developmentalism and Dialectics

Contemporary educational practice has been heavily influenced by developmentalism. Phase theorists advocating a developmental approach to human growth include thinkers such as Erikson, Piaget, Kohlberg, Fowler, and Evelyn and James Whitehead. The stages and phases of life as described by these approaches have been helpful in understanding the complexity of the human journey. Thus, there is merit in developmental approaches.

However, there are limits to developmental approaches. First, phase theorists because of their universalist tendencies sometimes err on the side of being too prescriptive thereby limiting personal experience and uniqueness. Secondly, proponents of stage development, by exaggerating the superiority of adults over children, are open to the charge of ageism (Beck, 1993, pp.96-97). Thirdly, developmentalists tend to be too linear in their approach and unappreciative of substantive evidence that much of growth in life is cyclical. Yet, despite these limitations, developmentalists do outline broad changes in human life that can assist in the human journey.

The two areas that I have attempted to weave in this work, contemplation and social action, have also been described from a developmental perspective. Some of the description has been helpful. Yet, cautions regarding developmentalism similar to those mentioned above need to be used with regard to phases in spirituality.

Within the Roman Catholic tradition a developmental approach has been used to understand the spiritual life. St. John of the Cross's 'Dark Night' and St. Teresa of Avila's 'Interior Castle' are considered classics in the spiritual way. They articulated three stages: the purgative, the illuminative, and the unitive. Groeschel, in *Spiritual Passages* (1983), has presented a detailed study of the psychological and spiritual aspects of these stages. However, he has continued a fundamental flaw in the Catholic tradition, which is to begin with the notion of sin. Bede Griffith has pointed out that this starting point ultimately results in a rejection of our real world.

> By placing the purgative ways first, this tradition gave a negative turn to the spiritual life with its emphasis on sin and redemption, while rejecting the positive values of the present world, of nature, the body, and the senses. (Fox, 1992, p.517)

This is an astute critique and helps to explain why it is often so difficult to discuss spirituality today. Traditional spirituality has tended to be negative and far from life affirming. The approach that I am advocating deliberately seeks to move away from a fixation on sin as the starting point and begin with the sense of wonder and the energy that comes from the contemplative sense of the 'tree with the lights on it'.

My approach is in keeping with the direction that Matthew Fox has taken. Fox argues that we need to see the spiritual life as including not three, but four stages. The first stage is the via positiva where we experience elation, awe, wonder, and delight. This is followed by the second stage, the via negativa, where we experience silence, letting go, suffering, sorrow, and grief. The third stage, the via creativa, is characterized by creativity, co-creating, life, and power. The fourth and final stage, the via transformativa, involves the work of justice-making. (Fox, 1991, p.18). Fox sees these phases as operating in a spiral fashion rather than a linear one and I tend to agree that this is more suitable for it permits gradual development as well as an on-going dialogue with different areas of our life.

While Fox is correct in the need to correct the traditional embeddedness in sin, I think that the same cautions that applies to the developmental approach itself need to be considered with regard to this four-fold method. That is, we must be careful of any tendency to universalize spiritual experience and to prescribe too closely what experience should be or will be. Moreover, we must be careful of falling into ageism and thereby leaving out certain age groups. Contemplation is innate to the human person and individuals regardless of age are capable of contemplating. Indeed, my experience with adolescents is that, when they are encouraged, they are very capable of looking at the world with open eyes and hearts.

We find in some praxis methods a developmental approach as well. Freire, for example, argues for four stages to the process of conscientization. The first stage, called the intransitive consciousness stage, refers to the level where there is a preoccupation with needs and a lack of historical consciousness. The second stage, that of semi-intransivity or magical consciousness, is the consciousness of closed societies. It is marked by a culture of silence where people take the socio-cultural facts as given. People tend to be defensive, dependent, and fatalistic. The third stage of naive or semitransitive consciousness is often called 'popular consciousness'. Here people begin to question, but at a naive and primitive level. People begin to see that humans create their socio-cultural circumstances. The political agency of people at this stage is weak in that they are often swayed by populist leaders. Finally, the fourth stage, that of critical consciousness, is, in Freire's view, the highest level of consciousness. It is achieved through the process of conscientization through dialogue and problematization. It is marked by refusal to accept dehumanizing structures and moves towards the union of action and reflection (Elias, 1976, pp.143-136).

> Learning for Freire is the process by which one moves from one level
> of consciousness to another. ... In other words, learning is the
> movement towards critical consciousness. (Elias, 1976, p.136)

However, Freire's conscientization process cannot be automatically transferred to our culture. Generally, in Canadian society people's basic needs are met and there is a fair degree of openness in Canadian society compared to other parts of the world. The result is that Canadians are generally critical of their leaders and exercise a fair degree of democratic action.

Hence, while there is merit in breaking up the conscientization process into different parts and to see them as sequential, we need to be cautious of being too prescriptive about people's learning. We can tend to limit the possibilities for people if we see them as in one stage as opposed to another. Undoubtedly, people do grow and mature in their consciousness and people do develop their ability to be reflective about their actions. However, we need to recognize that there are considerable variations within various stages and considerable overlap between them. This is due to the fact that every person is unique. Moreover, growth is more often cyclical than linear with the result being that people tend to re-visit previous learning periodically.

The dialectics of contemplation and liberating praxis requires that we integrate our active work for justice and our practice of contemplation. This dialectic is on-going and dynamic. There is a mutuality of support and correction so that the process of dialectics continues to move forward. Our contemplation deepens and expands. Our praxis becomes more effective. Setbacks in either dimension are embraced as learning moments. The dialectic approach tends to be more cyclical than linear as contemplation folds into action and action folds into contemplation. The movement is forward towards the future, but through a cycle of growth rather than a steady progress.

This being said, I think that the dialectic between contemplation and action does not negate the possibilities of stages or phases that developmentalists would advocate. The dialectic process simply points to the fact that learning is more complex than developmentalists would sometimes permit. Moreover, gender, age, race, or culture does not limit the process of contemplation-in-liberating praxis. It is a method for spiritual education that lends itself to varieties of locations and is more fluid and open than developmentalism. This is what makes it so valuable for education today.

Locations for Educating for This Method

I have been arguing that contemplation-in-liberating praxis is an appropriate spiritual method for our times. It stands upon the presumption that the human person is innately contemplative and innately active and that persons and communities achieve holism when these two dimensions are lived in an on-going dialectic. Because this method builds upon these presumptions it can be used with various ages, genders, races, and cultures. Nonetheless, despite the general application of this method, there are some distinctive concerns that support or limit the use of contemplation-in–liberating praxis. In particular some locations for education are more conducive than others.

In a general sense, formal institutions for learning, pre-schools, schools (primary and secondary), and post-secondary are often not conducive for a method that connects contemplation with liberating praxis. The reason for this is that formal educational institutions function more for the socialization of participants than for transformation of society.

> Instead of preparing students to enter the society with skills that will allow them to reflect critically upon and intervene in the world in order to change it, schools are conservative forces that, for the most part, socialize students to conform to the status quo. (Giroux, 1988, p.34)

Schools do serve in many ways to equip the young with the necessary skills and attitudes to function as responsible citizens within a complex world. However, when the concern for the appropriation of skills and attitudes for society as it is is not accompanied by a critique of the world, then schools tend to exist solely for the conservation of society. This approach tends to favor those who are benefiting from the way things are and to marginalize the concerns of those on the fringe of society. Moreover, it tends to discount a contemplative and a cosmological approach to learning.

The tendency of educational institutions to promote conservation rather than transformation is not limited to primary and secondary schools. It also resides at the post-secondary level. With regard to university education, bell hooks recognizes that "we inhabit real institutions where very little seems to be changed, ... almost no paradigm shifts, and where knowledge and information continue to be presented in the conventionally accepted manner" (hooks, 1994, p.143). Indeed, colleges and universities predominantly pursue conservative and/or liberal goals of professional accreditation and social adaptation rather than personal and social transformation.

Turning to the field of adult education David Smith has argued that even adult education, which claims to place praxis at the forefront, has been used in "helping people adjust to changes instead of enabling them to make changes" (Smith, 1995, p.115). In his view this is contrary to the goal of adult education which is participation in the creation of a "less exploitative and more cooperative kind of living" (Smith, 1995, p.116).

> Adult education should be busy in the process of helping people understand why we have food banks and what can be done about them, why we have endemic unemployment and what can be done

> about that, why we have sickness care instead of health care and what
> can be done about that, and so on. (Smith, 1995, p.125)

Adult education, as a location of learning, has fallen prey to "professionalization and psychologizing of the field" and it is this that has "prevented adult educationalists from seeing the importance of socio-historical" awareness in the construction of knowledge (Welton, 1987, p.7). Despite this difficulty, Welton argues that "adult learning is more central to societal reproduction, resistance, and transformation than that of children" (Welton, 1987, p.7). I agree with Welton and shall return to this point shortly.

Outside educational institutions and within the world of work we recognize the conservative forces under which most people have to work. The workplace rarely affords opportunity for transformative approaches especially when the area of spirituality is concerned. This may be simply because the world of work is so focused on doing rather than being (Whyte, 1994, p.19), that the possibilities for bringing an integrated spirituality to one's workplace is severely limited by that place. Some changes are occurring in some workplaces regarding the importance of spirituality for worker morale and for productivity. However, to date such changes are only tentative. The limitations of the workplace has led Margret Buchmann to observe that "the contemplative life and its potential closeness to the life of action depend on political and practical wisdom" (Buchmann, 1989, p.48). Hence, one must be both practical and wise should one seek to fully practice contemplation-in-liberating praxis where one works.

Now, conservative proponents tend to argue that education should be neutral and value-free and that bringing social and political questions into schools violates this neutrality. However, as Beck as argued, the neutral approach of trying to "sit on the fence in the matter of objectivity in politics" is wrong since we do have access to objectivity in politics (Beck, 1990, p.179). We have access to laws, political theories, voting trends, polls, and economic statistics, all of which can be brought to bear upon social, economic, and political education. A refusal to do so is to opt for indoctrination and to actually opt for a political stance that supports the status quo.

Crowe has argued that schools ought to be about encouraging personal creativity within the context of tradition (Crowe, 1985, pp.1-29). His concern is that students need a certain body of knowledge and an appreciation of history and tradition in order to situate their drive for creation and self-expression. This is certainly true. However, Crowe tends to be uncritical about the negative elements in traditions and sees them as the conditions for the possibility for creativity. A transformative approach to education would see tradition as limiting the possibility for change. It would call for a paradigm shift that involved a critique of tradition and a pursuit of alternative ways outside of the tradition.

Miller, Cassie, and Drake have proposed a tri-partite method of holistic education that would allow for the concerns of conservatives and liberals to be addressed while permitting the alternatives sought by transformative educators to be pursued as well. They argue that we need to allow for transmission, transaction, and transformation within learning. Transmission correlates with the conservative approach to education and focuses upon skills and social norms that students need so as to function in society. The transaction position roughly correlates with the liberal approach that focuses on problem solving within a democratic process. The transformation position focuses upon personal and social change (Miller, Cassie, and Drake, 1990, pp.3-6). This position would embrace contemplation-in-liberating praxis as a credible method. The three levels build one upon the other. A transformative approach requires the best of transmission and transaction so that those engaged can situate their concerns within a larger context. For example, contemplation-in-liberating praxis builds upon the history of contemplation and the contemporary attention to social and political structures and advances an alternative approach that moves beyond both of these.

As a result, despite the conservative nature of educational institutions it is possible and desirable that schools and post-secondary institutions pursue transformative approaches. Schools can be locations for the critique of society and for the promotion of alternative futures. The promotion of alternative and transformative approaches can be seen as part of the raison d'être of schools. "Schools can also be 'counter-cultural', challenging the dehumanizing elements of the dominant culture and proposing an alternative view." (De Roo, 1991, p.41) In light of this, contemplation-in-liberating praxis can be used in schools at different levels, particularly if attention is paid to the specific challenges and capacities of the students involved.

At the pre-school and primary level it is possible to facilitate the contemplative and active dimensions. Sofia Cavalletti, who based her work on Maria Montessori's method, argued plausibly that children have the capacity for wonder, awe, and contemplation. This capacity is nurtured through the judicious use of silence to help "the meditative spirit of the child" (Cavalletti, 1983, p.136). From her work with children aged three to six she speaks of wonder as proper to the child, poet, artist, and the old.

> Wonder is proper to the child, poet, artist and also to the old person who has known how to live by beholding and contemplating the world around him in such a way that reality has revealed ever widening horizons to him. (Cavalletti, 1983, pp.139-140)

Elsewhere, Jeffrey Pflaum has reflected on how he has used writing and music to help primary students develop their contemplative abilities (Pflaum, 1992, pp.6-12). The active dimension of liberating praxis can be facilitated through group actions like community clean-up days, multicultural days, exploration of roles and gender, visits to food banks, and similar activities. Thus, exposure to the issues of justice from within a cosmological perspective and in conjunction with the nurturing of contemplation, when done with respect to the age of the students, can provide an introduction to contemplation-in-liberating praxis spirituality.

Similarly, at the secondary school level, much can be done not only to introduce, but also to deepen, students' experience of contemplation-in-liberating praxis. My experience with adolescents is that they are quite open to practicing meditation. It is a bit exotic to them. I have used guided meditations frequently over the years and students have said that they found it quite helpful in bringing them a sense of peace. I have also used periods of silence, not for control, but to foster each person's mastery over his or her self. Silence, if introduced gradually (Palmer, 1983, p.82), can create an open and receptive climate in a classroom. Over the years I have developed an ease in discussing the importance of our emotions and our bodies with students as well as the importance of positive relationships and positive play for a balanced spirituality. Students tend, by and large, to see these as necessary and normal avenues for contemplative life.

Concerning the active dimension of liberating praxis I have found adolescents quite open to this area. Their natural idealism and the explosion of their critical capacities during the teen years lead them to be very open to the issues that are raised from within a cosmology of the earth as a community. More than their openness to critique is their openness to action. I have for several years run an Amnesty International Youth Group, the Terry Fox Run, a Fast to raise funds for the

Developing World, and frequently invited speakers into our school to discuss topics such as East Timor, Chiapas in Mexico, Peru, Canada's Native Peoples, and social welfare. Students enthusiastically take part in these activities for they are continually seeking ways to be active about creating a better world.

The times in which I have experienced the greatest success in integrating the contemplative with the active dimension of liberation in high schools has been in the context of a retreat. A retreat is composed of a special time and a special place in which retreatants reflect and learn about something of concern to them. A retreat allows times for silence and solitude, friendship and play, mediation and music. It also allows time for reflection on a social issue, for example world hunger. If the retreat involves an action, for example a fast to raise money, then the learning is heightened.

Beyond the retreat experience it is possible for students in a classroom to be exposed to the two dimensions of contemplation and liberating praxis. The extent and the success of the exposure often depend on the individual teacher and how comfortable they are with both areas. If teachers are contemplatives-in-liberating praxis, they will model this spirituality in their lifestyle and in their classroom practice. Maria Harris has argued that teachers need to contemplate the classroom environment, curriculum content, their teaching strategies, and their students and integrate such contemplation into their teaching (Harris, 1991, pp.25-29). It is important, then, that teachers contemplate and be socially and politically active.

Finally, to truly pursue contemplation-in-liberating praxis in a secondary school the support of the administration is necessary. Very often the strategies for promoting contemplation can seem unorthodox. Likewise, involving students in social and political issues can be controversial. In my experience, the support of the school administration can be of great assistance in this area.

Contemplation-in-liberating praxis can be taught and modeled for both primary and secondary level students. It can also be used at the post-secondary level. Jack Miller has documented his success with encouraging contemplation practice at the university level (Miller, 1994, pp.119-134). Except for the availability of time, I see little difficulty in postsecondary students learning and appropriating the contemplative-in-liberating praxis method. Indeed, they have ample opportunity to engage in both transformative action and reflection. Incorporating contemplation will simply add to their spirituality.

Moving outside formal educational institutions to the arena of adult education I see many possibilities for developing contemplatives-in-liberating praxis. I am not specifically thinking of adult education as the appropriation of employable skills.

> Whatever the interests of its academics, mainstream adult education practice in recent years has emerged as a professionalized, psychologistic pedagogy. (The designation of some, or most, of its activities as 'continuing education', or 'further education', or 'lifelong education', or 'recurrent education', does not alter the fact. These are the categories of modern adult education practice.) Increasingly, its concern has been with designing techniques that will change the individual learner's behaviour and inculcate coping skills to make up for what are claimed to be objectively identified deficiencies. (Collins, 1991, p.xi)

On the contrary, I am thinking of locations for adult education like the Antigonish Movement which "gave adult education a new dimension by making it an instrument of social change and reform" and " put new emphasis on cooperative education and gave cooperatives a social significance as well as an economic purpose" (Laidlaw, 1971, pp.74-75). Canadians have a long history of such adult education and are well respected within the international community. Canadian approaches to adult education have demonstrated a resourcefulness and a creativity that is studied worldwide (Selman, 1991, pp.44-47). Applying the best of adult pedagogy while being attentive to social, economic, and political realities has resulted in centers of communities for adult education that have been socially and politically effective. Canadians, then, have a history of success with regard to adult education for transformation.

As mentioned above I agree with Welton that locations for adult learning currently hold more transformative potential than locations with children and adolescents. Although adolescents have unbridled idealism, adults, in our society, have the power to initiate and sustain the actions necessary for social transformation. Conversely, however, while adults have more power, they tend to be under more constraints especially in the area of work. That is, if one begins to push for transformation there could be negative repercussions for one's job. This is not a negligible concern and it is a main reason, beyond the question of consciousness, for the inaction of many adults. Still, despite this limitation, adult learning locations are ripe sites for educating for contemplation-in-liberating praxis, especially if undertaken outside the workplace. Fox, for example, has pointed to the transformative impact of what he calls 'North American base communities': the Hospice Movement, Alcoholics Anonymous, Womenchurch, Dignity, Catholic Worker Houses, Deep Ecology Communities, and Professional Associations as Base Communities (Fox, 1991, pp.131-140). Wherever adults gather in small communities with the intention of promoting alternative ways of being to the dominant culture, contemplation-in-liberating praxis can be of benefit.

Adults, seeking to understand the complexity of our world within the framework of justice and cosmology while nurturing their spiritual life, will find in contemplation-in-liberating praxis a suitable method for learning. To the extent that they gather in learning communities with other adults we can envision communities on the road to liberation while supported by contemplation. Such communities could be seen as 'schools' in that they seek, create, and teach the knowledge that arises from being active contemplatives. These schools would be schools 'without graduates' where "real life is education, and becoming educated is real living" (Crowe, 1985, p.157).

Conclusion

Teaching is a rewarding, although at times difficult, occupation. I would go beyond Giroux in his claim that teaching is about intellectual work and argue that teaching is a work that engages the entire person of the teacher: intellectual, emotional, spiritual, communal, and active parts. Moreover, students who are caught up in the enterprise called learning must also be engaged in their entirety. The holistic demand of education is all the more evident when we turn to the area of spirituality. Indeed, in the area of spirituality we see clearly the place of vocation.

Viewing teaching as a vocation is not often appealed to these days for many different reasons including: scepticism regarding anything even remotely verging on the religious; a general denigration of those in public occupations, of which teaching is one; and the fact that so much of teaching has been reduced to technique and utility. However, we need to reclaim the use of the word 'vocation' for I think it points to a deeper and more comprehensive appreciation of what teaching and learning are all about.

> Vocation refers to a calling and entails firm commitment to the performance of worthwhile activities that are not merely calculated to advance personal career aspirations or fulfil minimum job expectations. It incorporates a strong ethical dimension, emphasizing

> an unavoidable necessity to make judgements about what should or
> should not be done and a readiness to take sides on significant issues.
> ... Vocation stresses personal responsibility on the part of the
> practitioner that cannot be abrogated by technicist prescriptions and
> preconceived formulations characterizing a cult of efficiency.
> (Collins, 1991, p.42)

It is in understanding the importance of both teaching and learning as being vocational moments that we can appreciate the kind of commitment that is called for when practicing contemplation-in-liberating praxis.

The concerns discussed in this chapter were raised to promote the practical ways and means of educating for contemplation-in-liberating praxis. The way of integrating contemplation and liberation seeks to speak to the vocational nature of teaching and learning. Indeed, it seeks to move educational practices beyond merely instrumental or pragmatic concerns to concerns of the spirit that apply to both our personal and collective realms. It requires a renewed commitment to education as a vocation wherein the promotion of the whole person and global justice are pursued together. Indeed, only with a keen sense of vocation can a person teach contemplation-in-liberating praxis for it is a work of the spirit.

CONCLUSION

> We are being carried along by a surge for meaning, which, contrary
> to many religious beliefs, is not drawing us away from the world but
> plunging us more profoundly into it, not alienating us from the divine
> but re-connecting us with the God who co-creates at the heart of
> creation. Not surprisingly therefore, the new spiritual search takes on
> global significance for many of its adherents.
>
> (O Murchu, 1998, pp.12-13)

Education is meant to be about a much grander project than the simple
accumulation of information and the application of a set of skills. In our
technological age seekers of information can easily find the data they want.
Moreover, in our rapidly changing world a person's skills are constantly in need of
reshaping, change, and renewal. In the midst of the swirling of new information and
the ongoing acquisition of appropriate skills a person needs to have a capacity for
being grounded in a sense of meaning and purpose so that they can live with a greater
sense of 'soul' or 'spirit'. This requires an education for a spirituality that meets the
needs of our age. My work is an attempt to articulate a method for spiritual education
that provides for the appropriation of meaning, purpose, and energy while at the same
time incorporating the socio-political realm. My proposed method is congruent with
a reconstructive postmodernism and is a method that has ecumenical and global
application.

Contemporary western education is biased against the promotion of
spirituality in general and particularly biased against a contemplative spirituality that
embraces social and political action. Our schools are too driven by a mechanistic and

rationalistic approach to learning. In fact, employment, rather than preparation for life, has become the raison d'être for Canadian public schools at the turn of this millennium. This stress on employment within formal education simply reflects preoccupation within Western culture with work, consumption, and wealth. Necessary as these are, these are too often pursued at the expense of the development of the whole person. What results are a diminished sense of well being and a fragmentation of life's energies. The result is a poverty of spirit within our culture.

This poverty of spirit is manifested in the personal realm by a lack of depth, creativity, and compassion. We notice this poverty of spirit in relationships that fail to satisfy, in the swift recourse to violence, in the hurried pace of life that more often than not leads to discord rather than peace. In the social and political realms this poverty of spirit is expressed in the injustices and inequalities that continue to plague our world. Western capitalism, for all its good, has yet to adequately address the crucial question of the just distribution of goods. Moreover, too little progress has been made to bring the concerns of women, minorities, the environment, and marginalized into the discourse of the mainstream. To the extent that these concerns have been ignored in spiritual discourses we can say that our spirituality has been impoverished.

As O Murchu has argued we need to discover new tools for discourse and to use a multi-disciplinary approach as we seek to reclaim the importance of spirituality today (O Murchu, p.13). Contemplation-in-liberating praxis is offered here as one such tool for discourse on education for spirituality today. While rooted in a traditional spiritual method it is new because it is available to those outside a theistic worldview and is future oriented through the incorporation of the political dimension. Moreover, to a certain extent this method is multi-disciplinary. It weaves critical pedagogy, philosophy, science, religion, history, and adult pedagogy into a method that can be used in a variety of disciplines and which can assist in a dialogue across disciplines. Finally, as a method available to peoples from different cultures and faith traditions it is an approach that has possible ecumenical and global applications.

Elsewhere, renowned religious educator Thomas Groome has proposed a method for spiritual education that has a wider appeal as well (Groome, 1998, pp.11-14). However, I differ from Groome in two fundamental ways. First, while I can appreciate the value of being rooted in a particular religion for the development of spirituality I believe it is time for a more humble discourse with non-religious persons who seek to bring their questions about spirituality to contemporary life. Secular humanists have much to teach about living a spiritual life and their insights can augment the ways of traditional religion if given a chance. Moreover, as eco-feminists have argued we need to bring the earth more directly into our discussions on spirituality. Appreciating the new cosmology of the earth as our common story can only serve to authenticate and challenge our spiritual discipline. Second, I am much more convinced that the political realm needs to be accentuated in spirituality today. Indeed, the concerns of politics and society will continue to impinge upon our consciousness, especially with the rapid advancement of communication technology and the growth of a global consciousness. This global consciousness will involve: a reclaiming of the importance of immanence along with transcendence; a valuing of holism along with specialization; and an appreciation of community along with solitude and action along with contemplation as integral to a spiritual life

Still, in the final analysis, no matter how good or innovative a method may be, the essential ingredient in education is the one who is called to teach. It is as Parker Palmer says, "good teaching cannot be reduced to technique; good teaching comes from the identity and integrity of the teacher" (Palmer, 1998, p.10). Hence, contemplation-in-liberating praxis requires teachers to be contemplatives engaged in liberating praxis. But in addition to this it is essential that such teachers be immersed in supportive learning communities where contemplative moments are valued as much as are actions for social and political change. Without such communities to support us on our spiritual journey, and in our educating for such a journey, we shall most certainly flounder. This would certainly be unfortunate for it would mean that those students who are open to this way would be deprived of the opportunity to begin to become contemplatives-in-liberating praxis.

Those of us who seek to deepen our own spiritual life while also pursuing peace and justice in our world need to be reminded that ours is a quest that integrates our personal needs with the needs of the earth and the global community. The deepening of personal spirituality today is so intimately connected with public justice in our global age that it is impossible to separate these two dimensions without damaging either. When these two dimensions are pursued dialectically energy is released that is creative and restorative for both individuals and communities. Contemplation-in-liberating praxis is one method for spiritual education that can facilitate the creation and restoration of a world worth living in and a world worth passing on to future generations. In light of this, contemplation-in-liberating praxis is a spirituality worth pursuing.

BIBLIOGRAPHY

Baker, James Thomas. *Thomas Merton, Social Critic*. Louisville, Kentucky: The University Press of Kentucky, 1971.

Barry, William A. and William J. Connolly. *The Practice of Spiritual Direction*. Minneapolis, Minnesota: The Seabury Press, 1982.

Baum, Gregory. *Religion and Alienation*. New York: Paulist Press, 1975.

_____. *Compassion and Solidarity: The Church for Others*. Toronto: C.B.C. Enterprise, 1987.

Beck, Clive. "Education for Spirituality" in *Interchange: A Quarterly Review of Education*. Toronto: OISE Press, Vol. 17, No.2, 1986.

_____. *Better Schools: A Values Perspective*. Great Britain: The Falmer Press. 1990.

_____. *Learning To Live The Good Life: Values in Adulthood*. Toronto: O.I.S.E. Press, 1993.

_____. "Postmodernism, Pedagogy, and Philosophy of Education" in *Philosophy of Education 1993: Proceedings of the Forty-Ninth Annual Meeting of the Philosophy of Education Society*. edited by Audrey Thompson. Urbana, Illinois: The Philosophy of Education Society, 1994.

_____."Postmodernism, Ethics, and Moral Education" in *Critical Conversations in Philosophy of Education*. edited by Wendy Kohli. New York and London: Routledge, Chapman, Hall, 1995.

Beck, Clive and Clare Madott Kosnik. "Caring for the Emotions: Toward a More Balanced Schooling" in *Philosophy of Education*, 1995.

157

_____ and Clare Madott Kosnik. "Care of the Soul in a Preservice Teacher Education Program" in *Holistic Education Review*. vol. 9, no. 3, September, 1996.

Bellah, Robert N, Richard Madsen, William M. Sullivan, Ann Swidler, and Steven M. Tipton. *Habits of the Heart: Individualism and Commitment in American Life*. New York: Harper and Row Publishers, 1986.

Benhabib, Seyla. "In the Shadow of Aristotle and Hegel: Communicative Ethics and Current Controversies in Practical Philosophy" in *Hermeneutics and Theory in Ethics and Politics*. edited by Michael Kelly. Cambridge, MA: M.I.T. Press, 1990.

Berry, Thomas. *The Dream of the Earth*. San Francisco: Sierra Club Books, 1990.

Bosacki, Sandra Leanne. "Theory of Mind and Education: Toward a Dialogical Curriculum" in *Holistic Education Review*. Vol. 10, No. 3, Autumn, 1997.

Boyd, Dwight. "Dominance Concealed through Diversity: Implications of Inadequate Perspectives on Cultural Pluralism" in *Harvard Educational Review*. vol. 66, no.3, Fall, 1996.

Brown, Alan. *Modern Political Philosophy: Theories of the Just Society*. London: Penguin Books, 1986.

Brown, Robert McAfee. *Spirituality and Liberation: Overcoming the Great Fallacy*. Louisville, Kentucky: The Westminster Press, 1988.

Brueggemann, Walter. *The Prophetic Imagination*. U.S.A.: Fortress Press, 1978.

Buchmann, Margret. "The Careful Vision: How Practical Is Contemplation in Teaching" in *American Journal of Education*. Vol. 98, No. 1, November, 1989.

Burghardt, Walter J. "Contemplation: A Long Loving Look at the Real" in *Church*. Vol. 5, Winter, 1984.

Butkus, Russell A. "Linking Social Analysis With Curriculum Development: Insights From Paulo Freire" in *The Journal of Religious Education*. Vol. 84, No. 4, Fall, 1989.

Callan, Eamonn. "Pluralism and Civic Education" in *Studies in Philosophy and Education*. Vol. 11, pp.65-87, 1991.

_____. "Finding a Common Voice" in *Educational Theory*. Vol. 42, No. 4, Fall, 1992.

Capra, Fritjof. *The Turning Point: Science, Society and the Rising of Culture*. New York: Simon and Schuster, 1982.

Carr, Anne E. *A Search for Wisdom and Spirit: Thomas Merton's Theology of the Self*. Notre Dame, Indiana: University of Notre Dame Press, 1988.

Cavalletti, Sofia. *The Religious Potential of the Child: The Description of an Experience with Children from Ages Three to Six*. preface by Jerome W. Berryman. trans. by Patricia M. Coulter and Julie M. Coulter. New York: Paulist Press, 1983.

Chittister, Joan D. *Heart of Flesh: A Feminist Spirituality for Women and Men*. Grand Rapids, Michigan: Eerdmans Publishing Company, 1998.

Chrisci, John. *Mysticism: The Search For Ultimate Meaning*. Lanham, MD: The University Press of America, 1986.

Collins, Michael. *Adult Education as Vocation: A Critical Role for the Adult Educator*. London and New York: Routledge, 1991.

Coward, Howard. "Religious Pluralism and the Future of Religions" in *Religious Pluralism and Truth: Essays on Cross-Cultural Philosophy of Religion*. edited by Thomas Dean. Albany, New York: State University of New York Press, 1995.

Crowe, Frederick E. *The Lonergan Enterprise*. United States of America: Cowley Publications, 1980.

_____. *Old Things and New: A Strategy For Education*. Atlantic, Georgia: Scholars Press, 1985.

Cully, Iris V. and Kendig Brubaker Cully, editors. *Harper's Encyclopedia of Religious Education*. San Francisco: Harper and Row, Publishers, 1971.

Dalai Lama. "Education and The Human Heart" in *Holistic Education Review*. Vol. 10, No. 3, September, 1996.

Daly, Herman E. and John B. Cobb, Jr. *For the Common Good: Redirecting the Economy toward Community, the Environment, and a Sustainable Future*. second edition. Boston: Beacon Press, 1994.

Dass, Ram and Paul Gorman. *How Can I Help?: Stories and Reflections On Service*. New York: Alfred A. Knopf, 1985.

Davis, Charles. *Soft Bodies in a Hard World: Spirituality for the Vulnerable*. Toronto: Anglican Book Centre, 1987.

Del Prete, Thomas. *Thomas Merton and the Education of the Whole Person*. Birmingham, Alabama: Religious Education Press, 1990.

De Roo, Remi J. "Teaching Social Justice in the Canadian Context" in *Catholic Education: Transforming Our World – A Canadian Perspective*. edited by Michael Higgins, et. al. Ottawa: Novalis, 1991.

Dillard, Annie. *Pilgrim At Tinker Creek*. New York: Harper and Row, Publishers, Incorporated, 1988.

Dunn, Stephen. "Ecology, Ethics, and the Religious Educator" in *The Journal of Religious Education*. Vol. 85, No. 1, 1990.

Dyckman, Katherine Marie and Patrick Carroll. *Inviting the Mystic, Supporting the Prophet: An Introduction to Spiritual Direction*. New York: Paulist Press, 1981.

Egan, Kieran. *Imagination in Teaching and Learning: The Middle School Years*. London, Ontario: The Althouse Press, 1992.

Elias, John L. *Conscientization and Deschooling: Freire's and Illich's Proposals for Reshaping Society.* Philadelphia: The Westminster Press, 1976.

Evans, Susan and Michael Dallaire. "God Calling Through Experience: The Church and the Poor" in *Challenging the Conventional: Essays in Honour of Ed Newbery.* edited by Wesley Cragg. Burlington, Ontario: Trinity Press, 1989.

Fenton, John Y. "Mystical Experience as a Bridge for Cross- Cultural Philosophy of Religion: A Critique" in *Religious Pluralism and Truth: Essays on Cross-Cultural Philosophy of Religion.* edited by Thomas Dean. Albany, New York: State University of New York Press, 1995.

Fox, Matthew. *Creation Spirituality: Liberating Gifts for the Peoples of the Earth.* New York: Harper Collins Publishers, 1991.

_____. *Sheer Joy: Conversations With Thomas Aquinas On Creation Spirituality.* foreword Rupert Sheldrake. afterward Bede Griffith. New York: Harper Collins, Publishers, 1992.

Freire, Paulo. *Pedagogy of the Oppressed.* trans. by Myra Bergman Ramos. New York: Herder and Herder, 1970.

_____. *Education: The Practice of Freedom.* London: Writers and Readers Publishing Cooperative, 1976.

Gadotti, Moacir. *Pedagogy of Praxis: A Dialectical Philosophy of Education.* preface Paulo Freire. trans. John Milton. Albany, New York: State University of New York Press, 1996.

Galbraith, John Kenneth. *The Culture of Contentment.* Boston: Houghton Mifflin Company, 1992.

Gilligan, Carol. *In A Different Voice: Psychological Theory and Women's Development.* Cambridge, MA: Harvard University Press, 1982.

Giroux, Henry A. *Teachers As Intellectuals: Toward A Critical Pedagogy of Learning.* intro. Paulo Freire, forword Peter McLaren. Granby, MA: Bergin and Garvey Publishers, Incorporated, 1988.

Givey, David W. *The Social Thought of Thomas Merton: The Way of Nonviolence and Peace for the Future.* Chicago, Ilinois: Franciscan Herdal Press, 1983.

Griffin, David Ray. "Introduction to SUNY Series in Constructive Postmodern Thought" in *Spirituality and Society: Postmodern Visions.* edited by David Ray Griffin. Albany, New York: State University of NewYork Press, 1988.

_____. "Introduction: Postmodern Spirituality and Society" in *Spirituality and Society: Postmodern Visions.* edited by David Ray Griffin. Albany, New York: State University of New York Press, 1988.

Groeschel, Benedict. *Spiritual Passages: The Psychology of Spiritual Development.* New York: Crossroad, 1983.

Groome, Thomas. *Educating For Life: A Spiritual Vision for Every Teacher and Parent.* Allen. Texas. Thomas More Press. 1998.

Gutierrez, Gustavo. *We Drink From Our Own Wells: The Spiritual Journey of a People.* foreword Henri Nouwen. trans. Matthew J. O'Connell. Maryknoll, New York: Orbis Books, 1985.

Haight, Roger. *An Alternative Vision: An Interpretation of Liberation Theology.* New York: Paulist Press, 1985.

Hall, Budd and Ed Sullivan. "Transformative Learning: Contexts and Practice". Toronto: O.I.S.E. Transformative Learning Centre, (working paper).

Hammarskjold, Dag. *Markings.* trans. Leif Sjoberg and W.H. Auden. London: Faber and Faber, 1964.

Hansen, Paul E. "Teacher As Prophetic Witness" in *Catholic Education: Transforming Our World – A Canadian Perspective.* edited by Michael Higgins, et. al. Ottawa: Novalis, 1991.

Hare, William. *What Makes a Good Teacher: Reflections on Some Characteristics Central to the Educational Enterprise.* London, Ontario: The Althouse Press, 1993.

Harris, Maria. *Teaching and Religious Imagination: An Essay in the Theology of Teaching.* New York: Harper San Francisco, 1991.

Holland, Joe. "A Postmodern Vision of Spirituality and Society" in *Spirituality and Society: Postmodern Visions.* edited by David Ray Griffin. Albany, New York: State University of New York Press, 1988.

Holland, Joe and Peter Henriot. *Social Analysis: Linking Faith and Justice.* Washington, DC: Center of Concern, 1980.

hooks, bell. *Teaching to Transgress: Education as the Practice of Freedom.* New York: Routledge, 1994.

Ibish, Yusuf and Peter Lamborn Wilson, editors. *Traditional Modes of Contemplation and Action: A Colloquium held at Rothko Chapel, Houston Texas.* Great Britain: Billing and Sons, Limited, 1977.

James, William. *The Varieties of Religious Experience: A Study in Human Nature.* intro. Reinhold Niebuhr. New York: Collier Books, 1961.

Jarvis, Peter. "Paulo Freire: Educationalist of a Revolutionary Movement" in *Convergence: International Journal of Adult Education.* Vol. 20, No. 2, 1987.

Johnson, Tony W. *Discipleship or Pilgrimage: The Educator's Quest for Philosophy.* Albany, New York: State University of New York Press, 1995.

Johnston, William. "Renewal in Mystical Theology" in *Religion and Culture: Essays in Honor of Bernard Lonergan, S.J.* edited by Timothy P. Fallon and Philip Boo Riley. Albany, New York: State University of New York Press, 1987.

Jung, Carl G. *The Development of Personality: Papers on Child Psychology, Education, and Related Subjects*. trans. R.F.C. Hull. New York: Princeton University Press, 1981.

Kamperindis, Lambros. "Surrounded by Water and Dying of Thirst" in *Parabola: The Magazine of Myth and Tradition*. Vol. xvii, No. 1, February, 1992.

Keller, Catherine. "Toward a Postpatriarchal Postmodernity" in *Spirituality and Society: Postmodern Visions*. edited by David Ray Griffin. Albany, New York: State University of New York Press, 1988.

Kelsey, Morton T. *The Other Side of Silence: A Guide To Christian Meditation*. New York: Paulist Press, 1976.

King, Alexander and Bertrand Schneider. *The First Global Revolution: A Report by the Council of the Club of Rome*. New York: Pantheon Books, 1991.

Knitter, Paul. "Cosmic Confidence or Preferential Option" in *Intercultural Challenges of Raimon Panikkar*. edited by Joseph Prabhu. Maryknoll, New York: Orbis Books, 1996.

Laidlaw, Alexander F., editor. *The Man from Mangaree: Writings and Speeches of M.M. Coady*. Toronto: McClelland and Steward Limited, 1971.

Lamb, Matthew. *Solidarity With Victims: Towards A Theology of Social Transformation*. New York: The Crossroad Publishing Company, 1982.

Lanzetta, Beverly J. "The Mystical Basis of Panikkar's Thought" in *Intercultural Challenges of Raimon Panikkar*. edited by Joseph Prabhu. Maryknoll, New York: Orbis Books, 1996.

Leddy, Mary Jo. "Exercising Theology in the Canadian Context" in *Faith That Transforms: Essays in Honor of Gregory Baum*. edited by Mary Jo Leddy, Mary Ann Hinsdale. New York: Paulist Press, 1987.

_____. "The Meaning of Catholic Education in a Post-Liberal Age" in *Catholic Education: Transforming Our World – A Canadian Perspective*. edited by Michael Higgins, et.al. Ottawa: Novalis, 1991.

Lonergan, Bernard. *Method In Theology*. New York: The Seabury Press, 1972.

Lorber, Michael A, and Walter D. Pierce. *Objective Methods and Evaluation for Secondary Teaching*. Englewood Cliffs, New Jersey: Prentice-Hall, Incorporated, 1983.

MacMurray, John. *The Self As Agent*. London: Faber and Faber, Limited, 1953.

Magana, Jose S.J. *A Strategy For Liberation: Notes for Orienting the Exercises Towards Utopia*. trans. Mary Angela Roduite. Hicksville, New York: Exposition Press, Incorporated, 1974.

McGowan, John. *Postmodernism and Its Critics: The Problem of Freedom in Postmodern Theory*. Ithaca, New York: Cornell University Press, 1991.

McKay, Alexander. "The Implications of Postmodernism for Moral Education" in *The McGill Journal of Education*. Vol. 29, No. 1, Winter, 1994.

Merton, Thomas. *New Seeds of Contemplation*. London: Burns and Oates, 1967.

_____. *Faith and Violence: Christian Teaching and Christian Practice*. Chicago, Illinois: University of Notre Dame Press, 1968.

Miller, John P. *The Holistic Teacher*. Toronto: OISE Press, 1993.

_____. *The Contemplative Practitioner: Meditation in Education and the Professions*. Toronto: OISE Press, 1994.

Miller, John P., J.R. Bruce Cassie, and Susan M. Drake. *Holistic Learning: A Teacher's Guide to Integrated Studies*. Toronto: O.I.S.E. Press, 1990.

Miller, Ron. "Holistic Education for an Emerging Culture" in *Holistic Education Review*. Vol. 10, No. 3, Fall, 1997.

Moffett, James. *The Universal Schoolhouse: Spiritual Awakening Through Education*. San Francisco, California: Jossey-Bass Publishers, 1994.

Moore, Thomas. *Care of the Soul: A Guide for Cultivating Depth and Sacredness in Everyday Life*. New York: Harper Perennial, 1992.

Mulligan, James. *Catholic Education: The Future Is Now*. Novalis: Toronto. 1999.

Noddings, Nel. *Caring: A Feminine Approach to Ethics and Moral Education*. Berkeley, California: University of California Press, 1986.

_____. *The Challenge to Care In Schools: An Alternative Approach to Education*. New York: Teachers College Press, 1992.

Nolan, Albert. *Contextual Theology: One Faith, Many Theologies*. Toronto: Regis College, 1991.

Nouwen, Henri J.M. *Thomas Merton: Contemplative Critic*. New York: Triumph Books, 1991.

O'Callaghan, Joseph F. translator. *The Autobiography of St. Ignatius of Loyola*. edited with introduction and notes by John C. Olin. New York: Harper and Row Publishers, 1974.

O'Donoghue, John. *Anam Cara: A Book of Celtic Wisdom*. New York: Harper Collins, Publishers, 1997.

Oliver, Donald W. with Kathleen Waldron Gershman. *Education, Modernity, and Fractured Meaning: Toward A Process Theory of Teaching and Learning*. Albany, New York: State University of New York Press, 1989.

O Murchu, Diarmuid. *Reclaiming Spirituality: A New Framework for Today's World*. New York. N.Y. The Crossroad Publishing Company. 1998.

Palmer, Parker J. *To Know As We Are Known: A Spirituality of Education*. San Francisco: Harper and Row, Publishers, 1983.

_____. *The Active Life: Wisdom for Work, Creativity, and Caring*. San Francisco: Harper Collins, 1990.

_____."The Grace of Great Things: Reclaiming the Sacred in Knowing, Teaching, and Learning" in *Holistic Education Review*, Vol. 10, No. 3, Fall, 1997.

_____. *The Courage to Teach: Exploring the Inner Landscape of a Teacher's Life*. San Francisco. Jossey-Bass Publishers. 1998.

Panikkar, Raimundo. *The Intrareligious Dialogue*. New York: Paulist Press, 1978.

_____. "The Contemplative Mood: A Challenge to Modernity" in *Cross Currents*. Vol. xxxi, No. 3, Fall, 1981.

_____. "Philosophical Pluralism and the Plurality of Religions" in *Religious Pluralism and Truth: Essays on Cross-Cultural Philosophy of Religion*. edited by Thomas Dean. Albany, New York: State University of New York Press, 1995.

Pead, Catherine M. *Bridges to Faith: The How and Why of High School Chaplaincy*. Ottawa: Novalis, 1991.

Peterson, Ralph. *Life in a Crowded Place: Making a Learning Community*. Richmond, Ontario: Scholastic Canada, Limited, 1992.

Pflaum, Jeffrey. "Contemplation Writing" in *Teachers and Writers*. Vol. 23, No.5. May-June, 1992.

Plunkett, Dudley. *Secular and Spiritual Values: Grounds for Hope in Education*. London: Routledge, 1990.

Price, James. "Typologies and the Cross-Cultural Analysis of Mysticism: A Critique" in *Religion and Culture: Essays in Honor of Bernard Lonergan, S.J.* edited by Timothy P. Fallon and Philip Boo Riley. Albany, New York: State University of New York Press, 1987.

Rajotte, Freda. "Justice, Peace, and the Integrity of Creation" in *The Journal of Religious Education*. Vol 85, No. 1, 1990.

Ricoeur, Paul. "Biblical Hermeneutics" in *Semeia*. Volume 4, 1975.

Rolheiser, Ronald. *Spirituality for a Restless Culture*. Mystic, Connecticut: Twenty-Third Publications, 1991.

Russell, Kenneth, C. "How Contemplatives Read the World" in *Spiritual Life: A Quarterly of Contemporary Spirituality*. Vol. 33, No. 4, Winter, 1987.

_____."The Contemplative Life: Barriers the Married Meet" in *Eglise et Theologie*. Vol. 15, 1984.

Sanford, John A. *Healing and Wholeness*. New York: Paulist Press, 1977.

Scherer, Margaret M. editor. *Educational Leadership*. Vol. 56. No. 4, December, 1998.

Schipani, Danial S. *Conscientization and Creativity: Paulo Freire and Christian Education*. Lanham, MD: University Press of America, 1984.

Selman, Gordon and Paul Dampier. *The Foundations of Adult Education in Canada*. Toronto: Thompson Educational Publishing, Incorporated, 1991.

Shannon, William. *Thomas Merton's Dark Path: The Inner Experience of a Contemplative*. New York: Farrar, Straus, Girioux, 1981.

Smith, David. *First Person Plural: A Community Development Approach to Social Change*. Montreal: Black Rose Books, 1995.

Soelle, Dorothee. *Political Theology*. trans. John Shelley. Philadelphia: Fortress Press, 1974.

_____. *The Strength of the Weak: Toward a Christian Feminist Identity*. trans. Robert and Rita Kimber. Philadelphia: The Westminster Press, 1984.

Street, James L. "A Shared Praxis Approach" in *The Journal of Religious Education*. Vol. 83, No. 2, Spring, 1988.

Sweet, Lois. *God In The Classroom: The Controversial Issue of Religion in Canada's Schools*. Toronto: McClelland and Stewart, Incorporated, 1997.

Taylor, Charles. *The Malais of Modernity*. Concord, Ontario: Anansi Press Limited, 1991.

Wallis, Jim. *The Soul of Politics: A Practical and Prophetic Vision for Change*. New York: Fount Paperbacks, 1994.

Welton, Michael R. editor. *Knowledge for the People: The Struggle for Adult Learning in English-Speaking Canada, 1828-1973*. Toronto: O.I.S.E. Press, 1987.

White, Stephen K. *Political Theory and Postmodernism*. Cambridge, England: Cambridge University Press. 1991.

Whyte, David. *The Heart Aroused: Poetry and the Preservation of the Soul in Corporate America*. New York: Currency Doubleday, 1994.

Willets, John W., Mary E. Boyce, and Carol Ann Franklin. "Praxis as a New Method in the Academy" in *Adult Learning*. Vol. 6, No. 5. May/June, 1995.

Winter, Gibson. *The Suburban Captivity of the Churches: An Analysis of Protestant Responsibility in the Expanding Metropolis*. New York: Doubleday and Company, 1961.

Woodman, Marion and Elinor Dickson. *Dancing In The Flames: The Dark Goddess in the Transformation of Consciousness*. Canada: Alfred A. Knopf, 1996.

✳

INDEX

✳

MELLEN STUDIES IN EDUCATION

14. Francis R. Phillips, **Bishop Beck and English Education, 1949-1959**

15. Gerhard Falk, **The Life of the Academic Professional in America: An Inventory of Tasks, Tensions & Achievements**

16. Phillip Santa Maria, **The Question of Elementary Education in the Third Russian State Duma, 1907-1912**

17. James J. Van Patten (ed.), **The Socio-Cultural Foundations of Education and the Evolution of Education Policies in the U.S.**

18. Peter P. DeBoer, **Origins of Teacher Education at Calvin Colege, 1900-1930: And Gladly Teach**

19. Célestin Freinet, **Education Through Work: A Model for Child-Centered Learning**, John Sivell (trans.)

20. John Sivell (ed.), **Freinet Pedagogy: Theory and Practice**

21. John Klapper, **Foreign-Language Learning Through Immersion**

22. Maurice Whitehead, **The Academies of the Reverend Bartholomew Booth in Georgian England and Revolutionary America**

23. Margaret D. Tannenbaum, **Concepts and Issues in School Choice**

24. Rose M. Duhon-Sells and Emma T. Pitts, **An Interdisciplinary Approach to Multicultural Teaching and Learning**

25. Robert E. Ward, **An Encyclopedia of Irish Schools, 1500-1800**

26. David A. Brodie, **A Reference Manual for Human Performance Measurement in the Field of Physical Education and Sports Sciences**

27. Xiufeng Liu, **Mathematics and Science Curriculum Change in the People's Republic of China**

28. Judith Evans Longacre, **The History of Wilson College 1868 to 1970**

29. Thomas E. Jordan, **The First Decade of Life, Volume I: Birth to Age Five**

30. Thomas E. Jordan, **The First Decade of Life, Volume II: The Child From Five to Ten Years**

31. Mary I. Fuller and Anthony J. Rosie (eds.), **Teacher Education and School Partnerships**

32. James J. Van Patten (ed.), **Watersheds in Higher Education**

33. K. (Moti) Gokulsing and Cornel DaCosta (eds.), **Usable Knowledges as the Goal of University Education: Innovations in the Academic Enterprise Culture**